1 MONTH OF
FREE
READING

at

www.ForgottenBooks.com

By purchasing this book you are eligible for one month membership to ForgottenBooks.com, giving you unlimited access to our entire collection of over 1,000,000 titles via our web site and mobile apps.

To claim your free month visit: www.forgottenbooks.com/free304799

ISBN 978-0-265-76327-8
PIBN 10304799

This book is a reproduction of an important historical work. Forgotten Books uses
state-of-the-art technology to digitally reconstruct the work, preserving the original format
whilst repairing imperfections present in the aged copy. In rare cases, an imperfection in
the original, such as a blemish or missing page, may be replicated in our edition. We do,
however, repair the vast majority of imperfections successfully; any imperfections that
remain are intentionally left to preserve the state of such historical works.

Building a Decision Support System:
The Mythical Man-Month Revisited

Peter G. W. Keen
Thomas J. Gambino

May 1980

CISR No. 57
Sloan WP No. 1132-80

Building a Decision Support System:
The Mythical Man-Month Revisited

Peter G. W. Keen
Thomas J. Gambino

May 1980

CISR No. 57
Sloan WP No. 1132-80

to appear as a chapter in Building Decision Support Systems, edited
by J. F. Bennett, Addison-Wesley Series on Decision Support.

TABLE OF CONTENTS

FIGURES

TABLE

1. Introduction

    1.1 Overview

    This paper describes the development of a Decision Support System, from its beginning as part of a research project through to the implementation of it as a commercial product used by six state agencies and public sector consulting groups. The system was designed by individuals with a long-standing involvement with DSS. As such, it provided an excellent opportunity to test the conventional wisdom on principles and techniques for DSS design.

    We had clear expectations as to what would be easy and what would be hard to implement. We wanted to see if the DSS field is at a stage where one can give builders reliable rules of thumb -- not a cookbook, but the sort of pragmatic advice that would be welcomed by a capable systems analyst, consultant or programmer setting out for the first time to deliver an interactive computer system to support decision makers in a complex task.

    ISSPA (Interactive Support System for Policy Analysts) is a DSS, written in APL, that supports administrators, analysts and researchers concerned with public policy issues $_{at}$ the state and local level. The initial application which this paper discusses is in the area of school finance: the funding of public education in individual states. However, ISSPA is of general relevance to planning and policy making in both the public and private sectors.[1]

    The development strategy was based on principles of adaptive design, derived from the recommendations of several researchers and practitioners (see Section 5).

These principles assume that the "final" system must evolve through usage and learning. Rather than focus on functional specifications, the designer relies on a prototype to:

(1) Find out quickly what is important to the user as opposed to what the designer thinks ought to be important;

(2) provide something concrete for the user to react to and experiment with; and

(3) define a clear architecture for the DSS, so that it can easily be modified and evolved.

The prototype is a real system, not a mock-up or experiment. It provides the base for learning-by-using.

As well as prototypes, adaptive design emphasizes:

(1) Careful attention to the user-DSS dialog, and thus to the design of the software interface;

(2) the importance of user learning, in terms of the evolution of the system and the need for flexibility in the DSS and responsive service by the system builders;

(3) getting started, rather than getting finished; and

(4) a command-based structure; ISSPA is built up of APL functions that directly correspond to the action words or the "verbs" users employ in their own problem-solving. A verb is a statement "do this", such as "give me descriptive statistics", which ISSPA performs with a DESCRIBE function.

1.2 The Mythical Man-Month

The adaptive design approach used with ISSPA, and the choice of

APL, reflect a hypothesis that is the main topic of this chapter:

> Adaptive design resolves the problem of the
>
> mythical man-month.

The mythical man-month is F.P. Brooks' summary[2] of the discrepancy be-
between the expected and actual effort required to develop software
products. Designers estimate the time for completion in terms of man-
months; their projections almost invariably turn out to be badly wrong
and the system often does not work.

Brooks identifies a number of explanations for the widespread
problems in planning for and delivering software systems. Assessments
of man-months are often based on the number of lines of code, However,
program coding is only 10% of the total effort. Moreover, if X is the
effort required to write and test a program, 3X is needed to make it
into a program product and 9X to integrate it into a system product
(Figure 1).

FIGURE I: Brook's Assessment of Relative Programming Effort

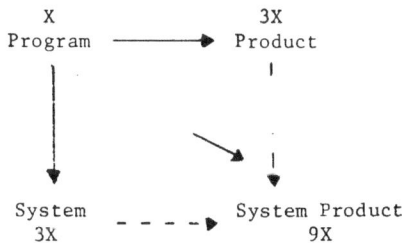

Making a program into a product involves documentation, additional
testing to ensure "robustness" (i.e., it should be able to handle inputs
and uses outside the range of the initial special-purpose program), error-
handling routines, etc. Integrating a program into a system requires

substantial testing of linkages, and often additional code must be
written to ensure consistency.

Brooks recommends several techniques to solve the problem of the mythical
man-month. He emphasizes the importance of a clear design architecture, the
use of "sharp tools" (including APL), and systematic testing procedures.

We were particularly concerned about the mythical man-month since we
wished to make ISSPA into a system product and had an extremely limited
budget. In essence, we started with a set of hypotheses about DSS development, in terms of adaptive design, system architecture, APL, and the
mythical man-month. The rest of this chapter describes our experiences,
focussing on the surprises. We found that:

(1) The principles of adaptive design, which are unique to
the DSS faith and stand in sharp contrast to the methods
of the systems development life cycle, hold up well.
Given APL as a tool, we have been able to evolve a complex
system out of simple components and respond quickly to
our users' changing needs.

(2) We underestimated the importance of having skilled users;
much of the testing process relies on them.

(3) While APL immensely speeds up the development process, it
has some hidden costs. It is extremely difficult, even
for expert programmers, to estimate the relative efficiency
of the source code. ISSPA is expensive to run and we
found that rewritting some sections of the code reduced
the processing cost by a factor of 20. We suspect that
many super-high-level languages share with APL a charac-
teristic we term opaqueness: the surface (the source code)
gives no clear indication of depths (machine-level).

(4) Brook's estimate of 9X seems to hold. Even with APL,
adaptive design and a highly skilled programmer, the
initial development effort has to be supplemented by
continuous attention to improving the usability of the
DSS. Of course, since APL reduces X, it also makes
the total effort -- 9X -- acceptable.

2. School Financial Policy Issues

Since the early 1970's, the funding of public schools has been
a major legislative and judicial issue in at least half the states
in the country.[3] The Serrano case in California (1973) established
that a child's opportunity for education -- expressed in terms of
expenditures per pupil in each school district in the state -- should
not be determined by his or her parents' and neighbors' wealth.
Towns with high wealth and property values can raise large revenues
for less effort than poor ones. Since local property taxes are the
major component of school revenues, this has resulted in huge dis-
parities between neighboring districts. To resolve this inequity,
the state must both limit rich districts' expenditures and provide
substantial aid to poor ones.

The main result of school finance reform has been to place
responsibility on the state legislature and executive to determine
the "formula", the set of precise equations on which each district's
state aid is based. This requires fundamental rather than incremental
analysis. A school district can base next year's plans on a budgeting
procedure which largely examines cost increases (especially in teachers'
salaries). The voters in the town will approve -- or, increasingly in
recent years, reject -- the budget. Similarly, in states where school
finance is not a major issue, the legislature can adjust last year's
formula, increasing the basic state aid by, say, 8%.

This incremental process, which has worked reasonably well for a century, breaks down when a judge declares the state's existing system unconstitutional or when school finance becomes a "hot" issue because of taxpayer revolts or when inflation affects the ability of local districts to raise adequate revenues. There must then be fundamental, not incremental analysis of policy choices.

Unfortunately, the professional staff responsible for such analysis can rarely provide it. The whole aim of ISSPA is to break through the technical constraints they face, but many organizational ones remain. The key problem is that the whole system has _always_ relied on incrementalism. There is no policy focus. Even when a court decision forces rethinking, legislators are mainly concerned with the "bottom line", the exact impact of a proposed formula on each of their constituent districts. This "costing out" of the formula leads to a narrow focus; the planning horizon is next year and longer-term qualitative issues are ignored.

The key issues in school finance concern data. It is a "numbers" game with lengthy arguments about who has the right figures. The state aid formula is generally based on a variety of data: attendance by grade, enrollment (which is not necessarily even close to attendance), local tax rates and revenues, transportation expenditures, special and vocational education information, etc., etc. School finance is a morass of numbers. In New York, for example, every local school superintendent must supply the state with up to 1,200 pages of data a year.

Control over this data is the major source of influence for the department of education, which is generally a poor step-child in state government. A few states have effective collection, control

and reporting procedures, but on the whole, the data management process
is clumsy and inefficient. There is a shortage of programmers. Low
salaries and lack of hardware, management and training mean the policy
analysts' major problem is access to high quality information.

These analysts are mainly legislative staff or professionals
working for executive fiscal and budget agencies. Their responsibili-
ties vary; they are partly watchdogs who monitor other parts of government (legislative or executive). They may initiate policy alternatives.
Above all, they evaluate information on the current state aid system
and on competing proposals for change. In general, the only computer-
based aids available to them are SPSS (the standard Statistical Package
for the Social Sciences) and limited batch "simulations" which do little
more than calculate what each school district would have received last
year had a proposed formula been used. Only a few states have more
advanced tools. These tend to be expensive but highly valued by their
users.

While legislative debates on school finance are limited to
incremental analysis and the bottom line, the policy issues are complex.
There is a rich research literature on measures of equity and alterna-
tive structures for a formula (foundation, guaranteed yield and pupil
weighting), and the field has an esoteric jargon -- recaptures, save
harmless, mills, and caps. The gap between the research concepts and
the practice of policy analysts is huge.

ISSPA is intended to bridge the gap, to provide analysts with a
"portable technology" that can help them add a real policy focus to
school finance. Since access to information is the key to effective
analysis, and even more, to influencing the legislative debate, ISSPA
is designed to allow fast and flexible manipulation and display of

information. It is a DSS for policy analysts not for policy analysis.

The state department of education often has a monopoly on data and data processing. It is also difficult for analysts to get appropriations for computer resources -- the centralized data processing unit can generally thwart local efforts to use other services. ISSPA had to be "portable". A portable technology is one that can be easily transferred and maintained. Portability includes:

(1) low cost; even $10,000 may be too expensive to justify, regardless of potential payoff -- if it involves a capital investment proposal and legislative approval;

(2) installation; given the frequent organizational isolation of analysts and the hostility of the data processing unit, it must be easy to build and update the ISSPA database and to bring up the DSS;

(3) ease of use and elimination of the need for training; the analysts have little experience with computers; it was important to make ISSPA self-explanatory;

(4) evolution; one long-term aim is to use ISSPA as a means of translating research concepts into analytic techniques. This means ongoing development; it is essential that users be able to get access to -- and contribute to -- the results.

Portability is as much a political as a technical concept.

3. ISSPA Design Features

    3.1 Introduction

    ISSPA is a command-driven system. There are five categories
of command:

>   (1) data management
>
>   (2) data manipulation
>
>   (3) data display and reporting
>
>   (4) statistical analysis
>
>   (5) user-system linkages (e.g., 'help' commands)

Conceptually, the database is a matrix in the form:

$$\text{planning units (rows x variables (columns))}^4$$

There is no fixed limit on either the rows or columns; ISSPA fills up
the workspace with variables (via the CHOOSE command) until it is full.
Labels for rows and columns may be of any length; users are not constrained to or muddled by uncommunicative mnemonics. In a typical
school finance application, the database contains 500-600 variables
for each of 500-750 planning units (school districts).

We deliberately chose a simple data structure and approach to
data management for ISSPA. Our assumption was that policy analysis
largely involves exploring and manipulating a small amount of high
quality data, and that analysts think of the data as a simple table
of values.

Commands in ISSPA are simple and kept as close to the users'
vocabulary as possible. Almost all DSS claim to be English-like, and
easy to learn and use. The evidence that ISSPA is indeed so is that
users have been able to operate the system, drawing on most of its
commands, with under an hour of training. The training is simply

a one-hour demonstration. There are currently almost 50 commands; the initial system, put into use seven months ago, contained 22. Table 1 lists the commands, with brief comments on how they evolved.

Considerable effort was put into the design of the user-system interface. Conventions were kept to a minimum. Most commands involve typing a single word, which is generally self-explanatory, such as LIST, PLOT, REGRESS, DEFINE or COUNTIF. A structured dialog is used within the more complex commands; ISSPA prompts the user, in a fixed sequence: "DO YOU WANT A OR B?"

The only conventions which take time to learn and use concern CHOOSing variables and variable identifiers. Since the database may be of any size, only a part of it can be in the workspace at any time. Users are told to view the DSS as a scratchpad. The commands operate on whatever is in the scratchpad. The user CHOOSEs which variables to bring in from disk (see Figure 2). We assumed that this would not be constrictive since users will rarely want, or be able, to deal with more than 10-20 variables at the same time (see also Morton, Carlson and Sutton).[5]

Labels and mnemonics for variables are cumbersome to use and hard to remember, especially since an ISSPA database often contains over 600 variables. The convention used in ISSPA is that variables are referenced by either a permanent identifier Vxxx, set up when the database is created, or by a temporary number Axx, showing the variable's location in the workspace ('A'xx = active variable number xx).

While analysts found their convention reasonably easy to accept, they still wished to define their own labels at least for those variables they used frequently. We added a SYNONYM facility so that now variables can be referred to by their V-number, A-number or a one-word user-supplied label.

TABLE 1: ISSPA COMMANDS

	(1) Library?	(2) Modify Dialog?	(3) Extend/ Improve?	(4) System Command?
1. Initial Commands				
CHOOSE/UNCHOOSE				
COMMANDS				x
CORRELATE	x			
COUNTIF				
CROSSTAB	x	x		
DEFINE/REDEFINE				
DESCRIBE				
DIRECTORY				
DONE				x
ENVIRONMENT				
FREQUENCIES	x			
HEAD				
HISTO	x			
LIST			x	
NTILES				
RANK			x	
REGRESS		x	x	
SCATTER				
TOP/BOTTOM				

2. Added when Version 0 made available to users

	(1)	(2)	(3)	(4)
ADD/DROP DATABASE				
CLEAR				
FORMAT				
GROUPIF/UNGROUP				
PARTIAL CORR	x			
RANGE, MIN, MAX, MEAN,				
MEDIAN, TOTAL				
SCALE/RESCALE				
WAVERAGE				

3. Added at user request

	(1)	(2)	(3)	(4)
COMMAND COST/SESSION COST				
CONTINUE		x		x
DISPLAY .... FOR UNITS				
SELECT UNITS		x		
SYNONYM				
VARS		x		x
WHAT IS				x
YEARS				
* SAMPLE				

4. User-defined   (1)   (2)   (3)   (4)

    OHIO

    WTILES

5. "Evolved" commands added by designers

    BOXPLOT

    CONDENSE

    EQUITY

    STEMLEAF

6. Extended Capability

    IMPS

(1) library? = taken from APL public library?

(2) modify dialog? = were substantial changes made to user-DSS dialog in response to user reactions?

(3) extend/improve? = were extensions or improvements made to the command, in terms of function not dialog?

(4) system command? = is this a general system command rather than user command?

FIGURE 2 - CHOOSING ISSPA VARIABLES

(User responses are underlined)

```
COMMAND: DIRECTORY
THE AVAILABLE DATA CATEGORIES ARE:
    1 ENROLLMENT
    2 REVENUE
    3 EXPENDITURES
    4 STAFF
    5 TAX BASE AND TAX RATE
    6 DISTRICT CHARACTERISTICS
EXPLORE ANY GROUP ('NO')?    ENROLLMENT
V101  TOTAL ADM 79
V102  TOTAL ADM 78
V103  SPECIAL EDUCATION ADM 79
V104  SPECIAL EDUCATION ADM 78

EXPLORE ANY GROUP ('NO')?    2
V201  TOTAL REVENUE 79
V202  TOTAL REVENUE 78
V203  LOCAL REVENUE 79
V204  LOCAL REVENUE 78
V205  STATE BASIC AID 79
V206  STATE BASIC AID 78
V207  SPECIAL EDUCATION AID 79
V208  SPECIAL EDUCATION AID 78
V209  OTHER REVENUE 79
V210  OTHER REVENUE 78
```

```
COMMAND: VARS

• • •NO ACTIVE VARIABLES• • •

COMMAND: CHOOSE
GROUP OR ITEM?    GROUP
GROUP NAME (STOP)?    ENROLLMENT
GROUP NAME (STOP)?    STOP

CURRENT NUMBER OF ACTIVE VARIABLES:  4
```

```
COMMAND: VARS
THE ACTIVE VARIABLES ARE:
A1  V101  TOTADM79      TOTAL ADM 79
A2  V102  TOTADM78      TOTAL ADM 78
A3  V103  SPECEDADM79   SPECIAL EDUCATION ADM 79
A4  V104  SPECEDADM78   SPECIAL EDUCATION ADM 78
```

```
COMMAND: CHOOSE
GROUP OR ITEM?    ITEM
ENTER VARIABLE (V) NUMBER ('STOP'):?    V201
ENTER VARIABLE (V) NUMBER ('STOP'):?    V301
ENTER VARIABLE (V) NUMBER ('STOP'):?    STOP

CURRENT NUMBER OF ACTIVE VARIABLES:  6
```

(1) DIRECTORY lists variable groups in the permanent database

(2) V101 is permanent numeric identifier number, and TOTAL ADM 79 its permanent discriptor

(3) Group 2, REVENUE, has 10 variables

(4) the workspace is currently empty

(5) CHOOSing the ENROLLMENT group results in four active variables

(6) an active variable may be referenced by its A-number, V-number or synonym (user-supplied) to, (e.g., A1, V101 or TOTADM79) may be used interchangeably with any command

(7) CHOOSE individual variables rather than a group

```
COMMAND: VARS
THE ACTIVE VARIABLES ARE:
A1   V101   TOTADM79       TOTAL ADM 79
A2   V102   TOTADM78       TOTAL ADM 78
A3   V103   SPECEDADM79    SPECIAL EDUCATION ADM 79
A4   V104   SPECEDADM78    SPECIAL EDUCATION ADM 78
A5   V201   TOTREV79       TOTAL REVENUE 79
A6   V301   TOTOPEXP79     TOTAL OPERATING EXP. 79
```

```
COMMAND: RANK V201,V301,V101 BY V101
*PP*
```

(8) Sample Command
RANK A5, A6, A1
by A1 would have
same effect

			TOTAL REVENUE 1979	TOTAL OP. EXP 1979	TOTAL ADM 1979
1.	0301	BIG CITY S.D.	186,951,769	171,591,450	99,219
2.	0501	CAPITOL CITY S.D.	130,481,187	109,444,927	80,330
3.	0101	RIVER CITY S.D.	92,870,956	85,310,671	56,970
4.	0502	INDUSTRY CITY S.D.	83,791,031	64,457,113	46,897
5.	0204	LANCASTER CITY S.D.	13,337,333	9,871,846	7,514
6.	0206	XENIA CITY S.D.	10,415,333	8,324,413	6,608
7.	0102	LAKOTA LOCAL S.D.	8,507,302	6,396,336	6,474
8.	0104	ZANESVILLE CITY S.D.	9,310,625	6,963,875	5,810
9.	0503	BEDFORD CITY S.D.	13,490,072	9,250,840	5,717
10.	0208	TROY CITY S.D.	7,319,274	5,213,457	4,766
11.	0103	MIAMISBURG CITY S.D.	7,061,369	5,365,450	4,347
12.	0205	LOGAN CITY S.D.	4,787,049	3,924,081	4,036
13.	0201	ELIDA LOCAL S.D.	3,856,170	2,996,168	3,137
14.	0202	GALLIA COUNTY LOCAL	4,852,539	3,949,600	3,041
15.	0203	LAKEVIEW LOCAL S.D.	3,328,556	2,650,652	2,230
16.	0209	THREE RIVERS LOCAL	4,189,051	2,867,830	2,030
17.	0403	MIAMI EAST LOCAL S.D	2,153,682	1,623,376	1,623
18.	0207	WINDHAM EX VILL S.D.	2,388,170	1,623,665	1,586
19.	0102	BEACHWOOD CITY S.D.	6,025,259	4,347,745	1,535
20.	0504	GRANDVIEW HEIGHTS	2,926,374	2,157,401	1,341
21.	0401	LISBON EX VILL S.D.	1,619,886	1,317,526	1,339
22.	0401	HUNTINGTON LOCAL S.D	1,302,025	1,172,409	1,250
23.	0106	MONROEVILLE LOCAL	1,207,650	865,555	771
24.	0105	WOLF CREEK LOCAL S.D	977,054	885,322	704
25.	0210	NEW KNOXVILLE LOCAL	635,392	472,290	395

We allowed variable names to be of any length, to ensure that reports would be meaningful and clear. If users -- or the legislator or public interest groups for whom they prepare analysis -- think of a variable as "GUARANTEED YIELD, GOVERNOR'S PROPOSAL", then that is what must appear on reports, not "GY, GVR". Obviously, by providing maximum flexibility on variable labels, we had to find a compact and efficient (from the user's perspective) mode of reference.

3.2 Program Structure

The program structure of ISSPA is relatively simple in concept. There are three separate components (See Figure 3):

(1) User-system interface;

(2) commands ("LIST", "REGRESS", etc.); and

(3) data management routines, transparent to
     the user.

Most of the initial effort went to defining the interface, which handles the dialog between the users and the system and thus strongly determines if they will view the DSS as friendly and easy to use. Once the initial system was released for use, significant effort was needed for the data management routines. Many of the commands use APL functions from public libraries (see Section 6), especially those for statistical analysis.

Brooks draws attention to the "architecture" of a system. The command-based structure we used for ISSPA meets many of his recommendations:

(1) It reflects a top-down approach and the dialog-manager is
     independent of the commands and data management routines;

(2) each command is fully independent of the other; a new one
     can be added to ISSPA with no change to the logic of the
     dialog manager or to any other command;

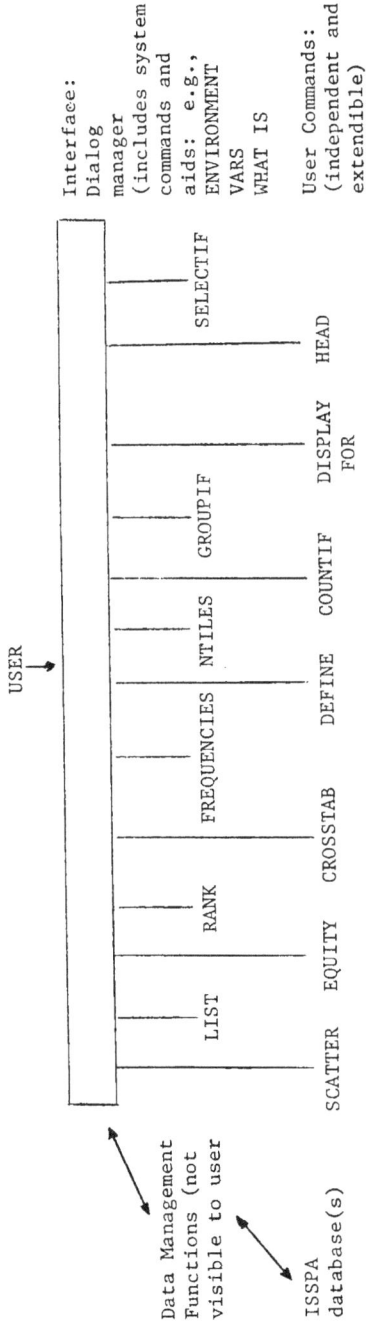

FIGURE 3: ISSPA PROGRAM STRUCTURE

(3) our design methodology is a form of "stepwise refinement".
     We implemented an initial version of a routine and refined
     it on the basis of users' experiences and reactions.

The convention for naming variables illustrates this last point.
We started by deciding that there would be no restrictions on variable
labels for reports. This meant that the label could not be used as
the variable **indentifier,** since this could mean typing 50 characters or
more. We struggled to **defin**d a compact method and initially tried the
V-number approach. We added A-numbers to deal with variables defined
from other variables (e.g., DEFINE (V101 + V109) ÷ V217).

The initial system was used for several months before we extended
it. We added (Figure 4):

(1) SYNONYM;

(2) WHAT IS; to allow easy identification of a variable;

(3) IDENTIFIER: this lists the full label for any A-number,
     V-number or synonym;

(4) VARS; this shows the identifiers for all the variables
     currently active.

Adaptive design assumes that such extensions will be added <u>as a
direct result of system usage.</u> One cannot predict in advance exactly
what will be needed. The early users of ISSPA in effect taught <u>us</u>.

4. The Development Process

4.1 Introduction

This section briefly summarizes the sequence of the development
process. Adaptive design is based on rules of thumb. We present the
rules as we proceed and list them at the end of the narrative.

FIGURE 4: IDENTIFYING VARIABLES IN ISSPA

(User Inputs Underlined)

(1) SYNONYM   V404

CURRENT SYNONYM: LOCAL TAX BASE

NEW SYNONYM: LOGT

SYNONYM   A11

NO CURRENT SYNONYMS

NEW SYNONYM: FEDTAX79

(2) WHAT IS   TOTENRL78

A1   V102   TOTENRL78   TOTAL ENROLLMENT 78

(3) IDENTIFIER   A1

TOTAL ENROLLMENT 78

(4) <u>VARS</u>

THE ACTIVE VARIABLES ARE:

A1	*V201*	*TOTREV79*	*TOTAL REVENUE 79*
A2	*V301*	*TOTOPEXP79*	*TOTAL OPERATING EXP. 79*
A3	*V101*	*TOTENRL79*	*TOTAL ENROLLMENT 79*
A4		*SURPLUS79*	*OPERATING SURPLUS* (DEFICIT) 1979

The initial system took roughly 70 hours of effort on the part
of the programmer (Gambino). Keen, in an ongoing research study,
had spent six months studying the design and use of the computer models
and information systems in state government agencies concerned with
school finance policy making. The computer systems available to policy
analysts in most states were cumbersome and very limited in scope.
The analysts complained of their lack of flexibility and of the unavail-
ability of data. Generally, they were unable to get programs written
to produce special reports; the data processing staff were unresponsive,
overworked or incompetent. A few states had useful interactive systems,
but these were expensive ($200,000 - $1,000,000).

The initial design aim for ISSPA was to show that a simple, general,
flexible and cheap DSS could be built that would meet the analysts'
needs and also facilitate better and more extensive exploration of
policy issues. Limited funds were available for the initial system.
From the start, however, ISSPA was intended to be a system product
in Brooks' sense of the term; it was expected that there would be
sufficient demand for such a system that funds would be available for
continued development.

The development fell into three distinct phases:

(1) Phase 1: build the initial system, Version 0.

(2) Phase 2: extend it, adding new commands and improving
existing ones in response to users' reactions.

(3) Phase 3: create the system product that is portable,
stable and documented.

Each phase posed different challenges.

FIGURE 5:   EQUITY COMMAND

```
COMMAND: WHAT IS V101,A37,A38
A1    V101    TOTADM79        TOTAL ADM 79
A37           REVPERPUPIL     $ REVENUE PER PUPIL
A38           EXPPERPUPIL79   $ EXPENDITURES PER PUPIL 79


COMMAND: EQUITY A37,A38 BY V101
ENTER PERCENT FOR 'PERCENT MEAN' CALCULATION:?   50
ENTER 'E' VALUE FOR 'ATKINSON'S INDEX' CALCULATION?   .5
•PP•
                        PER PUPIL       PER PUPIL
                         _1979___        _1979___

NO. OBS. (N)                  25               25
RANGE                     2,885.           1,896.
RESTRICTED RANGE            557.             729.
FED RANGE RATIO             0.420            0.728
REL. MEAN DEV.              0.090            0.120
PERMISSIBLE VAR.            0.874            0.866
WEIGHTED VAR.            55,264.          51,486.
COEF. OF VAR.               0.107            0.142
STD. DEV. OF LOGS           0.124            0.156
GINI COEF.                  0.059            0.080
PCT. MEAN                  99.6             99.6
ATKINSON'S IND.             0.996            0.994

COMMAND: EQUITY A37,A38
'BY' MUST BE USED WITH 'EQUITY', E.G. EQUITY A1 BY A2

COMMAND:
```

(1) (pp = position paper;
system pauses till
carriage return hit)

(2) "by" variable is
weighting factor
used to compute
measures requiring
weighting population

4.2 Phase 1: The First Meeting

At their first meeting, Keen and Gambino began by sketching out
the user-system dialog. Keen, as the analyst, had a clear idea of
the initial set of user verbs to be supported. For example, it was
obvious that analysts relied heavily on rankings; e.g., they would
create a report listing expenditure figures, with the district with
the largest average revenues per pupil showed first. This became a
command: "RANK .... BY".

Keen presented the verbs and Gambino suggested the exact dialog.
Keen would respond to the recommendation; generally, it would be
rejected if it was cumbersome or clumsy for a non-technical, inexperienced
user.

The meeting lasted three hours. There was a constant give-and-take
between analyst and technician. A general dialog was agreed on but
not set in concrete. This dialog determined the nature of the data
management routines. We had started by focussing on the representation
of the data; it must appear to the user as a simple table of values.
Each command must operate directly on the table, with no specific procedures needed on the part of the user to get, manipulate or update data.

It is worth noting that our approach was the opposite of standard
systems analysis. We began from the outputs and worked back to the inputs, leaving the procedures to be specified later. This reflects our
view that what happens at the terminal determines the "quality" of the
DSS; to the user, the interface is the system. Most programmers focus
on defining the input data and then the procedures, leaving the outputs
to last.

This strategy also allowed Gambino, who was completely unfamiliar
with school finance, to quickly learn a great deal about the intended

users. Many programmers have a naive view of the user. Indeed, the "user" is often only an abstraction. From the start, all our design effort emphasized what the user would say and see. The "quality" of the DSS was defined in terms of ease of use, lucidity and gracefulness. Far from being an abstraction, the user was a real presence.

This initial phase of the development process reflects a key and reliable rule-of-thumb:

Rule 1: Design the dialog first. Forget about input files, functional capabilities, etc.:

R.1(a): Define what the user says and sees at the terminal.

R.1(b): Define the representation of the data: what does it look like to the user?

4.3 Initial Commands

Keen distinguishes between usefulness and usability in a DSS.[6] Usefulness relates to the capabilities of the system: models, retrieval facilities and report routines. Usability refers to the user-system dialog. Our first rule of thumb stresses usability. Obviously, though the initial system has to contain something worth using.

The link between users' verbs and DSS commands is a key one for our design strategy (see Section 6). Understanding the user involves identifying his or her verbs. The verbs provide design criteria for the commands that constitute the useful components of ISSPA. We defined two types of command:

(1) Those based on generic verbs; and

(2) those that are special-purpose.

Generic verbs are the ones common to most problem-solving and analysis, and that are required in most DSS. For example, any task involving data analysis needs a LIST, RANK and HISTO (gram) command. We identified a dozen generic commands, most of which could be provided with minimal programming.

Generic commands will already have been implemented in other systems. We chose to use APL partly because excellent public libraries are available on several computers. APL is a convenient language for borrowing routines since integrating them into a program requires very little effort. All the statistical routines in ISSPA come from public libraries. We have found that 2-8 hours are required to modify, integrate and test a routine from a library. Since it has already been at least partially, and in most cases entirely, debugged, we save much of the 9X of effort Brooks identifies. The main modifications needed in adding a function to ISSPA involve the user-system dialog. Many of the designers of APL programs show little sensitivity to the user (see Section 7).

Most special-purpose commands obviously must be programmed. For policy analysis in general, we identified well over 20 special-purpose verbs and for school finance another 10. The general verbs largely related to statistical techniques and measures and the school finance ones to measures of equity and approaches to comparing and ranking school districts.

Examples of the various types of command we identified for potential inclusion in the initial version are:

(1) generic: LIST, RANK, DESCRIBE (descriptive statistics), HISTO (gram), DEFINE (new variable), FREQUENCIES, ADD (to) DATABASE.

(2) special-purpose:

    (a) policy analysis: SELECT UNITS, COUNTIF, BOTTOM, NTILES, GROUP, REGRESS, ANOVA

    (b) school finance: EQUITY, (equity measures), GINI, LORENZ[7]

We put priorities on the commands. This was done informally and based on four criteria:

(1) The <u>priority to the user</u>; i.e., the extent to which this command reflected a verb the analysts rely on or would immediately find useful;

(2) <u>ease of implementation</u>; HISTO and REGRESS could be taken directly from an APL public library;

(3) <u>clarity of user-DSS dialog</u>; with REGRESS, we could lay out in advance a simple complete dialog. We found it hard to do so for ANOVA (analysis of variance) and thus left that for a later version; and

(4) <u>likelihood of acceptance</u>; we avoided trying to force unfamiliar or contentious routines on the user; we could -- and did -- add them later.

The focus on user verbs and the use of a command-based program structure were an effective and simple technique. Our ability to extend version 0 from 12 to 50 commands directly resulted from these rules of thumb:

<u>Rule 2</u>: Identify the users' special-purpose verbs.

<u>Rule 3</u>: Identify generic verbs, relevant to this DSS.

<u>Rule 4</u>: Translate the verbs into commands, and vice versa.

<u>Rule 5</u>: Check public libraries for off-the-shelf routines, especially for generic verbs.

Rule 6: Set priorities for implementing commands for version O.

Rule 7: Support first, extend later; aim at giving the user something he or she will readily accept and add the less familiar, more complex capability later.

4.4 Version O

A working system was available within 40 hours.[8] It contained the following user commands:

LIST, DESCRIBE, RANK, TOP, BOTTOM,

HISTO, REGRESSION, CORRELATE and NTILES

(e.g., 10 NTILES = deciles, 4 NTILES - quartiles)

The regression, histogram and correlation routines were taken from a public library. Version O included other commands needed to manage the user-system dialog or improve the usability of the DSS; e.g., DIRECTORY, CHOOSE, ENVIRONMENT.

When the preliminary system was ready, we spent substantial time (10 hours) improving what the users saw on the terminal. The major changes that needed to be made concerned the formats of the outputs. Whereas functional specifications involve laying out a report format in some detail, adaptive design is similar to the concept of stepwise refinement. Instead of asking users "What do you want?", we said "How do you like this?".[9]

We entirely redesigned the dialog and style of the outputs by playing with the system, prior to showing it to potential users. After an additional 20 hours of programming effort, we had an operational system (70 hours in total), with over 30 commands. This was made available to a senior policy analyst and his assistant in a large state's education agency. Over the next three months, they worked with the system and many extensions and modifications were made (see 4.5 below).

This first phase of development worked out well. Even at commercial rates for programming and computer time, we had spent under $4,000. We demonstrated the system in several states; instead of trying to sell an idea, we could show a complete working DSS. We kept careful track of the development process up to this stage; we wanted to check our experience with the general conclusions of Ness, Courbon et al., and Grajew and Tolovi.[10] We agree with Grajew and Tolovi's estimate that the initial system, which will then evolve through usage, can be built for under $10,000 in less than 16 weeks.

This is an important point, since:

(a) It reduces the user's risk and encourages experiment; a DSS becomes more of an R&D effort than a capital investment; and

(b) the lead time between the initial proposal and a usable system is short enough that the users' enthusiasm and momentum are not dissipated.

Version 0 was simple but not simplistic. The analysts who saw it were impressed by how easy ISSPA is to use and by its power:

Rule 8: Keep it simple from the start; aim for a few useful commands for version 0 and evolve a complex DSS out of simple components.

Rule 9: Deliver version 0 quickly and cheaply.

Rule 10: Make sure version 0 sells itself; it must be easy to use, the outputs clear and the dialog self-explanatory.

4.5 Phase 2: Bringing in the Users

In a sense, potential users of ISSPA were involved from the start. Keen's and Clark's studies of school finance had included surveys and interviews with analysts, legislators and administrators in eleven states. They discussed the idea of ISSPA with several experienced analysts, who worked with version 0 and played a major role in the evolution of ISSPA.[11]

We were extremely selective in looking for potential users. Since version 0 was intendedly only a start and not the final system, the skills and creativity of the early users would strongly influence the quality of the full system. Adaptive design relies on good users.

Our first user was a widely-respected senior analyst in a large mid-western state. He was impressed with ISSPA and, with the help of a subordinate who had some knowledge of computers, began using it after one demonstration. There was no user manual: while this led to occasional problems, ISSPA is largely self-explanatory.[12]

We wanted the initial users to react to ISSPA and to test it. We did not want them to have to debug it. Debugging means finding errors; testing, in our sense, means seeing how well the system works, deciding what needs to be changed or added and, above all, critiquing the quality of the interface.

Version 0 was not bug-free. We had left the complex issue of data management till last. We had carefully designed the representation of the data -- how it looked to the user. As we built the data management routines, we introduced errors; what worked on Monday bombed for no apparent reason on Tuesday.

In retrospect, we should not have released version 0 until we had implemented a reasonably complete initial version of these routines. Some users get very unhappy very quickly with an unstable system. (However, they are also very tolerant of errors in the first release of a new command.)

As we expected, we learnt a lot from the early users. One episode was instructive. NTILES is a command that identifies the cutpoints that break the distribution of values into equal groups; e.g., 5 NTILES REVENUES lists quintiles, 10 NTILES deciles, etc. This was an obvious command to include in version 0, since in school finance court cases and legislative reports, a frequent comparison is made between, say, the top 10% and the bottom 10% of school districts. We assumed that the NTILES command would be seen by analysts as helpful, but not unusual.

In fact, NTILES was enough in itself to sell the merits of ISSPA. In most states, calculations of deciles are done by hand. SPSS, the standard statistical package analysts use, does not allow observations to be reordered. In several states, we found instances where COBOL programs had been written to print the 5%, 10%, 25%, 33%, ... 95% intervals for a distribution, but only for specified variables. The idea that such programs could be generalized and on-line access provided came as a surprise to many analysts.

Once the analysts had access to a general routine like NTILES, they used it in new ways and developed new ideas from it. For example, WTILES adds an equity measure to the simple deciles or quantiles NTILES provides (WTILES stands for Weighted NTILES). It allows the analyst to answer such questions as "What are the 1978 expenditures for the bottom 10% and bottom 90% of the students in the state?". The analyst who defined WTILES used it as the basis for a major report on school finance equity and felt that the analysis could not have been done previously.

The sequence of events summarized above occurred several other times. The general pattern was:

(1) Data processing had provided a specific solution to a
    specific problem;

(2) we identified the <u>general</u> verb relevant to the problem;

(3) we provided a flexible command;

(4) use of the command stimulated a distinctive new idea
    or approach; and

(5) we added the resulting <u>user-defined</u> command to ISSPA.

We strongly feel that this pattern is a central aspect of DSS
development. Keen studied over 20 published case descriptions of
DSS and concluded that in many instances, the most effective uses of
the systems were both entirely different from the intended ones and
could not have been predicted beforehand (see Section 5).[13] Learning and evolution of system commands are a natural outcome of adaptive
design.

Such learning requires skilled users. Throughout the second phase
of the development of ISSPA, we found the users' role to be central;
we had not anticipated their importance in testing. At one stage, we
had users in five separate states. One of them was of immense value
to us, one was close to a disaster. We feel sure that the experience
provides a general lesson to DSS builders. Adaptive design provides
a working system quickly. <u>The designer realizes that there will be many
things wrong with it and gains immensely from the users' reactions.</u> If
the users are not highly skilled in their own job and actively interested
in the DSS, the designer does not get essential feedback.

A "working" system is one that has no <u>obvious</u> bugs. "*!39VW" or
"SYNTAX ERROR" is clearly a bug, but $210 instead of the correct $160
is not. Because a DSS is intendedly a flexible tool, under the user's
control, it does not have a set of "correct" inputs, procedures and

outputs. Even in a standard data processing application, it is
impossible to test all combinations. Flexibility, generality, ad hoc
uses, and variety of inputs, commands and outputs compound the problem.
Only a good user can alleviate it. User A (the good one) provided
invaluable feedback. User Z either did not recognize errors or simply
complained that "something's wrong"; the credibility of ISSPA suffered
as a result. In several instances, legislators were given incorrect
reports. The errors were subtle and only an expert on school finance
could spot them. User Z was, reasonably enough, very bothered when
errors were revealed but did little to uncover or cure them. User A
sought them out.

What we learned from all this was that a distinguishing aspect
of DSS development is that it is user-dependent:

(1) Adaptive design is an interactive process of learning
and feedback between a skilled user and a skilled
technician.

(2) the user tests a DSS;

(3) many DSS bugs are unobtrusive and remain dormant
until a user finds them;

(4) the range of functions exercised depends on the user.
Bugs reveal themselves only by use. Only an imaginative,
confident, involved user gives the DSS an adequate
work out.

Rule 11: Pick a good user; look for someone who:

(a) has substantial knowledge of the task the
DSS supports;

(b) has intellectual drive and curiosity;

        (c)   will take the initiative in testing and in

               evolving version 0; and

        (d)   enjoys being an innovator.[14]

 During this second phase of development, ISSPA grew in scope and sophistication. Very few commands were left unchanged; many of the improvements were minor enhancements in formatting or ease of use. New commands were added that were specific to school finance (i.e., not based on generic verbs). For example, EQUITY (see Figure 5) provides 12 measures of the equity of an existing or proposed state aid plan. It is derived from a research paper by Berne[15] which has had substantial influence on school finance policy research but little on policy making. Whereas the initial commands supported analysts' existing processes, EQUITY was specifically intended to add something new.

    Gerrity introduced the concept of descriptive and prescriptive mapping of a decision process in DSS development.[16] The descriptive map identifies how the task is currently handled; our focus on user verbs is one approach to doing so. The prescriptive map provides a long-term direction for improving the process. It reflects a normative concept, often derived from theory and research.

    Keen and Clark had identified as major shortcomings in existing policy analysis a lack of any real focus on strategic issues, long-term forecasting and conceptual models.[17] Berne's research on equity measures was too far from most analysts' experience and interests for them to apply it. By embedding the easy-to-use EQUITY command in ISSPA, we could encourage them to adopt a broader approach to policy issues. We explicitly viewed ISSPA as a way of bringing policy research to policy making.

We did not force analysts to use EQUITY. It is one of many resources available in the DSS. Since it involves typing a single phrase, there is minimal effort involved in trying it out. Keen argues that a DSS is often a way of making useful models usable.[18] We took Berne's 12 measures -- the useful component -- and made them accessible. Once we had a complete and stable system, more and more of our effort went into commands like EQUITY which extend rather than support the user. Figure 6 shows three commands, BOXPLOT, STEM and LEAF and CONDENSE, taken from Tukey's Exploratory Data Analysis (EDA).[19] They required very little programming effort[20] and some of our users are unaware they exist; they are an unobtrusive method for stimulating learning. Rule 7 stated: support first, extend later. For a DSS to be more than a convenience, it obviously must go beyond LIST, RANK, DESCRIBE, etc. At the same time, unfamiliar concepts and routines must be presented in a simple way. We did not define an EQUITY model or an EDA package. The verb-based architecture provided an easy bridge between usefulness and usability.

4.6 Phase 3: Building a System Product

Phase 3 involved converting ISSPA from a system to a product. Users were now buying a DSS. We had to provide technical support, documentation and training. Increasingly, we were concerned with costs. APL programs are not inexpensive to run. We had expected ISSPA to cost $50 an hour on the excellent system we were using. The actual figure was closer to $200 an hour. We found that APL penalizes careless pro- gramming very heavily indeed. Unfortunately, however, whenever we improved the efficiency of the programs, users were able to do more work in a given time, so that our cost per hour increased. We hired a group of APL

FIGURE 6:   EDA COMMANDS

1. BOXPLOT;   displays distribution of values for variable(s)

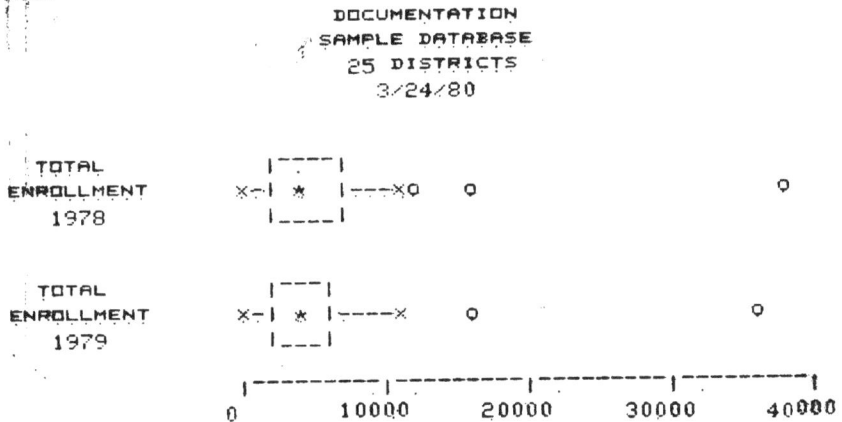

```
COMMAND: BOXPLOT TOTENRL78, TOTENRL79
PPP.

                            DOCUMENTATION
                            SAMPLE DATABASE
                             25 DISTRICTS
                               3/24/80


   TOTAL               | ---- |
ENROLLMENT         x-|  *   |----x0    0                          0
   1978               | ____ |


   TOTAL               | --- |
ENROLLMENT         x-|  *  |----x    0                        0
   1979               | ___ |

                   |---------|---------|---------|---------|
                   0        10000     20000     30000     40000
```

* = median

box shows lower and upper quartiles

---- = interquartile distance

x = lowest and highest data values falling within line
    which is same length as the interquartile distance
    extended from lower and upper quartiles

0 = values outside the above range

♠ = values falling more than 1.5 interquartile distances
    from lower and upper quartiles

2. STEMLEAF: stem-and-leaf plot

    (1) divides range of data into intervals of fixed
         length (a scale factor may be specified)

    (2) stem is vertical line, with interval boundary
         (0-3) shown to left

    (3) leaf is second significant digit of data value
         e.g., enrollment of 13,000 has stem of 1 and
         leaf of 3, 2,000 has stem of 0 and leaf of 2

    (4) leaves are sorted and shown in ascending order

```
COMMAND: STEMLEAF TOTENRL78
SCALE FACTOR: 2
.PP.


TOTAL ENROLLMENT 78

00|01111
00|2222233
00|445
00|6667
00|89
01|1
01|3
01|
01|6
01|
02|
02|
02|
02|
02|
03|
03|
03|
03|
03|9
.PP.

VALID CASES:    25
MISSING CASES:   8
```

(3) CONDENSE: summarizes distribution of values

```
COMMAND: CONDENSE TOTENRL78, TOTENRL79
STATISTICS ('ALL','STOP'):?    ALL
.PP.
```

	TOTAL ENROLLMENT 1978	TOTAL ENROLLMENT 1979
NO. OBS. (N)	25.	25.
MINIMUM	410.	395.
LOW 8TH	1,370.	1,338.
1ST QUARTILE	1,608.	1,585.
MEDIAN	4,057.	4,035.
3RD QUARTILE	6,773.	6,608.
HIGH 8TH	10,859.	10,127.
MAXIMUM	38,720.	37,365.
MIDSPREAD	5,165.	5,023.

See Tukey, J. Exploratory Data Analysis, Addison-Wesley,
    1977, for a discussion of the use of these techniques
    McNeil provides APL and FORTRAN routines for EDA.
    The ISSPA routines do not use his code. Outputs
    from McNeil's version of CONDENSE is shown below.

    (McNeil, D. R., Interactive Data Analysis
    (Wiley-Interscience, 1977))

experts who were sure they could halve the cost per hour. They were unable to do so. From this, we could conclude that with APL, the code gives little idea of the run time.

Efforts to use desk tops and minicomputers to reduce cost were amusing but ineffectual. With an IBM 5100, run time went from seconds to hours. Even with an HP-3000, we reduced costs by a factor of five and increased response time by twenty. Every improvement in the cost effectiveness of hardware improves DSS capability. However, current technology is still inadequate in providing fast and cheap and easily developed and flexible systems.

Whereas in Phase 1 we were concerned with the process of developing a DSS, in Phase 3 we had to shift our attention to the system product. The transition is expensive. Over a four month period, we added few new user commands but spent almost 800 hours on programming. The effort went into:

(1) improved data management routines;

(2) overlaying functions to reduce cost;

(3) user-system commands, such as:

    (a) SESSION COST: How much have I spent so far?

    (b) WHAT IS Vxxx: What is the label for V?

(4) new commands demanded and often defined by users; it is worth noting that in most cases, the commands represented new ideas and approaches stimulated by ISSPA; and

(5) user documentation, including a comprehensive manual.

As we expected, data and data management became a key issue. Policy analysis generally involves both operational data, such as historical figures on expenditures, program levels and budgets, and

planning data, which is often not available from routine sources.
We deliberately limited the data management capabilities in ISSPA and
required users to provide us with a single tape containing "clean" data.
This in effect provided a barrier to entry; if a state lacks capability
in data collection or if reliable, current historical data are not
available, it makes no sense to provide an interactive DSS to process
bad data more quickly and in more detail. McCoubrey and Sulg provided
us with a useful decision rule: "Assume the data do not exist, no
matter what Data Processing tells you.".

Creating an ISSPA database is technically very simple. Even so,
we encountered a variety of irritating minor problems, many procedural.
Even with operational data pulled directly off computer tapes, there
is some manual link needed. We had to provide a variety of facilities
for error checking, and for updating, correcting and adding to the
database. Obviously, a generalized database management system would
have helped, especially by reducing the manual work required. However,
it was, and still is, an infeasible option. DBMS requires a maturation
in the use of computers, financial investment and level of technical
competence that state governments (and, in our experience, many mid-
sized private businesses) lack.

We found that most of the complicated programming for ISSPA went
into minor functions for data management. Moreover, we were unable to
provide the same responsive service to users in this area that we boasted
of in anything involving ISSPA commands. If a user wanted a special
analytic routine, we could provide it overnight. Whenever there were
problems with a command, the difficulty was invariably easy to resolve,
since it was localized. A disadvantage of having data management be
"transparent" to the users was that when an error occurred, they had no

idea what was going on -- and at times, neither did we. (Transparent means that users are kept unaware of the dynamics or complexity of the system operations; everything "happens" without effort on their part.) The error often affected several user commands.

We found no guidance in the DSS literature, which provides little discussion of data management. None of our problems were complex or hard to resolve, but we found, increasingly:

(a) Programming effort was diverted from user commands to system functions;

(b) processing time and inefficiencies increased as we tackled data management issues; for example, we often had several duplicate copies of matrices to keep track of in the workspace; and

(c) our simple data structure in matrix form (from the user's view) and vector form (the physical structure) was still the best solution. The dilemma for DSS design is that since uses are varied and unpredictable (Section 5), there is no optimal physical or logical structure. Complex data management procedures greatly add to system overhead.

The whole issue of data management in DSS is a complex one, and we could find little help that translated into reliable rules of thumb. Carlsen describes a methodology for data extraction that is powerful but expensive.[21] In general, techniques for ad hoc modeling are far ahead of those for ad hoc data management, especially with large data bases. In Gerrity's PMS and GADS, a DSS developed at the IBM Research Laboratory,[22] most of the programming effort and computing resource was needed for data extraction: pulling from a large permanent database the relatively small subset of variables needed for a given user command. We could not have afforded such overhead; the price we paid was an imbalance between the responsiveness, low cost and flexibility of our analytic commands and the limited, slightly cumbersome nature of our data management routines.

Rule 12: Recognize that data management, not commands (or models) are binding constraint on DSS development:

(a) choose as simple a representation as possible (e.g., a matrix); and

(b) avoid complex data extraction and manipulation.

4.7 Conclusion

ISSPA is now (early 1980) a commercial product. It has to compete in a market that is very cost conscious. Users also expect instant service. Whereas at the end of Phase 1, we were ready to write a paper on the mythical man-month defeated, now we are not so sure. APL, and the middle-out strategy and a command-driven architecture provide immensely powerful techniques for developing a DSS. However, extending a working system to a system product is a complex process, with many hidden costs. For example, there is no quick or cheap way to produce a good user manual. In Phase 1, we were able to "sell" the system through explanation and hands-on experiment, because we were personally credible with our users. By Phase 3, the manual was needed to establish the credibility of ISSPA.

Figure 7 lists our 12 rules of thumb, with two more added:

FIGURE 7:   RULES OF THUMB FOR BUILDING DSS

RULE

1.   Design the dialog first:

- define what user says and sees

- define representation of data

2.   Identify user's special-purpose verbs

3.   Identify generic verbs relevant to this DSS

4.   Translate verbs into commands, and vice versa

5.   Check public libraries for off-the-shelf routines

6.   Set priorities for implementing commands for Version 0

7.   Support first, extend later

8.   Evolve complex DSS out of simple components

9.   Deliver Version 0 quickly and cheaply

10.   Make sure Version 0 sells itself

11.   Pick a good user:

- has substantial knowledge of task

- has intellectual drive and curiosity

- will take initiative in testing and evolving,
Version 0

- enjoys being innovator

12.   Recognize data management is main constraint, not commands

13.   Remember Brooks is right

- programming is 10% of effort

14.   Know your user at all times

Rule 13: Remember Brooks is right.

Rule 14: Know your user at all times.

Rule 13 may be restated in several ways:

(1)　programming is 10% of the effort;

(2)　if you want to build a product that will stand by itself, recognize the time and effort needed; and

(3)　Version 0 can be built in weeks.

Rule 14 reflects the whole logic of adaptive design. Of all techniques for applying computer-based models and information systems to complex decision processes, Decision Support involves the most attention to the user as a real person. At every single step in the development of ISSPA, our success depended on:

(1)　supporting a person, not solving a problem or building a model;

(2)　getting feedback from analysts' direct use of the DSS; and

(3)　responding to users' ideas and requests.

5.　Principles of Adaptive Design

5.1　Introduction

A recurrent theme in DSS research is user learning.[23] A DSS does not solve problems, but lets individuals exploit their own skills in problem-solving. The obvious strategy for DSS design is to support first, extend later; the initial system is close enough, in terms of commands and mode of dialog, to the users' current procedures to be both attractive and easy to use. Clearly, however, if the DSS is to stimulate changes in the decision process, learning has to occur.

Keen (1979) draws attention to a consistent finding in DSS case studies: the unpredictability of system uses. The actual uses of a DSS are frequently entirely different from the intended ones. For example, Gerrity's Portfolio Management System, intended to support the investment decision, became instead a valuable aid to marketing and communicating with customers. Often, the most innovative and valued uses of a DSS could not have been anticipated by the designer.

Keen summarizes this process, which has substantial implications for the choice of a design architecture and an implementation strategy, in a framework that views -- in fact defines -- a Decision Support System as an adaptive development strategy applicable only to situations where the "final" system cannot be predefined, but must evolve through the interactions of user, system and designer. Figure 8 shows these adaptive influences.

This conceptual framework was developed partly from a review of DSS research and case studies and partly through the process of developing ISSPA. It translates into some very specific design criteria and techniques. Most importantly, it views user learning as a direct outcome of DSS usage and a contributor to it. The explicit reason for building ISSPA was to help improve policy analysis; learning was viewed as the central issue for design and usage.

5.2 The Cognitive Loop

Each arrow in Figure 8 indicates an adaptive influence. System → User, for example, indicates that the DSS stimulates changes in the user's problem-solving process. If an interactive system does not require or aim at such user learning, then the label DSS is superfluous. Keen argues that it is meaningful to label a system a DSS only if doing so leads to a different development strategy than would otherwise have been chosen.

FIGURE 8:   AN ADAPTIVE DESIGN FRAMEWORK FOR DSS

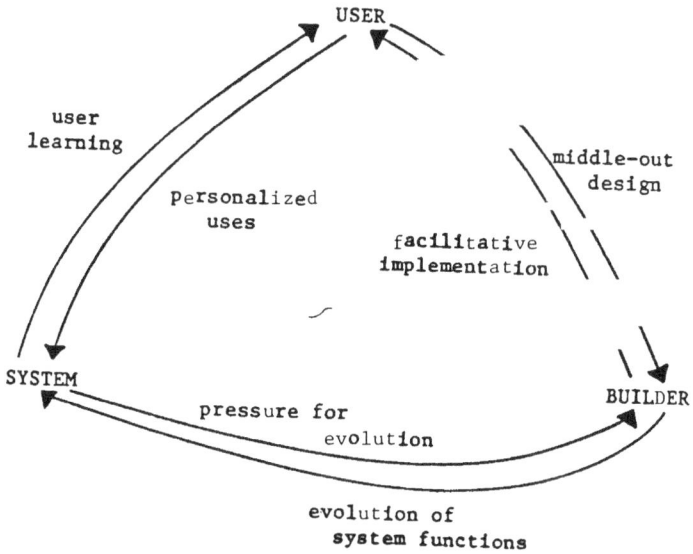

Situations where a system cannot be predefined and used independent
of the choices and judgments of the user, and where it will be extended
and modified, require a distinctive development process in which learning, adaptation and evolution are central.

The interactions between the user and the system directly relate
to learning. The DSS is intended to stimulate changes in user thinking: at the same time, it must be flexible enough to adapt to the
user as these changes occur. New tools must shape new uses, and vice-
versa. As the user develops a new approach to problem-solving, he or
she must not be constrained by the previous one. If.a system follows
a rigid sequence of routines, learning is blocked. The User $\longrightarrow$ System
link thus relies on a design architecture that permits personalized
use; without it, any learning stimulated by the DSS cannot be exploited.

5.3 The Implementation Loop

Keen terms the user-system links, the cognitive loop.
The implementation loop refers to the relationship between the designer
and the user.

Ness defined a key aspect of adaptive design: "middle-out"
development.[24] This is contrasted with top-down or bottom-up approaches,
and relies heavily on fast development and prototyping. Middle-out
design provides a means for the designer to learn from the user
(User $\longrightarrow$ Designer). While the concept of adaptive design is somewhat
broader than middle-out, Ness's concepts are at its core.

The implementation process requires a facilitative strategy on
the part of the designer (Designer $\longrightarrow$ User). A DSS is not an off-the-
shelf product. Building it requires close involvement with the user.
Several researchers have commented on the need for an intermediary (Keen)

or integrating agent (Bennett) who can act as a crusader, teacher and
even confidant.[25] Adaptive design is a joint venture between user and
designer. Each needs to respect and understand the other. The designer's
job goes well beyond traditional systems analysis and functional
specifications. He or she needs to:

(1) understand the task and user;

(2) be able to humanize and even customize the system; and

(3) be responsive to the user and help stimulate exploration
and learning.

In most instances of successful DSS development, the system is
associated with a skilled intermediary/implementer. The DSS is as
much a service as a product.

5.4   The Evolution Loop

The evolution loop relates to the process by which learning,
personalized use, middle-out and facilitative implementation combine
to make the initial system obsolescent and evolution essential. This
is shown in Figure 8 as an adaptive link from system to designer.
Evolving the system means adding new commands (Designer ⟶ System).
Knowing when and how to evolve it requires keeping track of user and
usage   (System ⟶ Designer).

The main value of the command-based architecture used in ISSPA
is that it is easy to add commands, given APL. The DSS designer has
to **plan** for evolution. Since many of the new commands will be user-
defined, they may be very different from the preceding ones. Obviously,
however complex or esoteric they may be, it is essential that they do
not involve restructuring the program, only adding independent modules
to it. Brooks describes the need for "conceptual integrity" in the
architecture of a system

"The purpose of a programming system is to make a
computer easy to use .... Because ease of use is the purpose,
(the) ratio of function to conceptual complexity is the
ultimate test of good system design ....

For a given level of function, however, that system
is best in which one can specify things with the most
simplicity and straightforwardness."[26]

Evolving a DSS relies on conceptual integrity. The command-
based, top-down structure of ISSPA provides for this. A major
postulate of the adaptive design framework is that a DSS is a
vehicle for user learning and hence, that evolution is inevitable
and essential.

Knowing when and how to evolve the DSS is often difficult. In
the initial stages of development, there is usually close and direct
contact between Designer and User. Later, however, the designer will
need a more formal methodology for tracking usage. The obvious one
is a data trap which records, with users' permission, each command
they invoke. These records may be analyzed in terms of mode of use,
reliance on individual commands, and stringing commands together into
distinct sequences or sentences. A data trap can provide a wealth
of information to the designer. However, there is no easy way of
interpreting it. (Stabell, Andreoli and Steadman provide one approach,
used to evaluate Gerrity's Portfolio Management System.)[27]

5.5 Adaptive Design in ISSPA

The descriptive mapping of the ISSPA users' decision process was
done by Keen and Clark, with a view towards defining ways to improve
analytic capability in school finance policy analysis.[28] It was clear
that analysts most want, and know how to use, simple, reliable data.

Whereas in statistical analysis they focus on medians, averages and correlations, they are also concerned with measures of range and variance, and with outliers. For example, they often need to look at extremes, such as the lowest and highest 10% of districts in terms of tax revenues per pupil. Their role is frequently to explain issues to legislators, and respond very quickly to their requests for analysis.

The descriptive mapping identifies the key issues in making a DSS usable. The prescriptive map defines how to make it more useful. Our analysis was similar to Gerrity's and Stabell's assessment of the Portfolio Management System. We found that the analysts had fairly simple concepts of policy analysis and relied on only a few techniques, especially ranking and linear regression. The descriptive map for a DSS focusses on how people carry out a task. The prescriptive map looks at the task itself. Gerrity found a lack of analytic concepts among portfolio managers. There is a rich body of financial theory relevant to their job that they do not draw on. They do not base their decisions on analysis of their customers' portfolios, but think in terms of individual stocks, ignoring issues of risk-return trade-offs. The school finance analysts similarly ignore policy research; they think incrementally and rarely go beyond the discussion of the bottom line. They focus on very few overall policy issues.

Gerrity built PMS to support the existing process and move users towards a more analytic one. Stabell found that the intended change did not occur and argued that not enough attention was paid to how to stimulate learning. With ISSPS, we intended to evolve the system by adding commands that reflected concepts new to the analysts. For example, we hoped to introduce adaptive forecasting techniques, incorporate research on equity measures and encourage sensitivity

analysis and exploratory data analysis. Clearly, it is unlikely that
analysts subject to organizational traditions and pressures of day-
to-day operations, will spontaneously adopt these new approaches. We
needed some leverage point and decided that the key issue for stimulating
learning is to find a really good user. Our assumption, backed up by
the findings from DSS case studies is that skilled users, helped perhaps by capable intermediaries (Designer → User in Figure 8), will
explore the DSS, find personal ways of using it (User → System), provide the design team with insights and challenges (User → Designer)
and respond to recommendations and training (Designer → User). In
this way, they themselves will help the system evolve.

We viewed ISSPA specifically as a vehicle for stimulating user
learning. We expected that:

  (a)   initially users would rely on fairly simple commands,
reflecting simple user verbs;

  (b)   as they got used to the DSS and found it valuable,
they would string these together into sentences, reflecting a methodology for analysis; once this occurred,
we would need to provide an "exec" facility; and

  (c)   they would then ask for extensions to existing commands,
define new ones and be ready to try out ones such as
EQUITY.

The principles of adaptive design indicated that for this sequence
to occur (as it did), we had to ensure that the development process
allowed all the adaptive links to operate:

  (1)   for the cognitive loop, this meant:

    (a)   the interface and dialog must be communicative,
responsive and easy to use and the commands directly

relevant to the existing process, to facilitate
use and learning (System ⟶ User). (We have no
formal measures of the quality of these features
of the interface; the number of user errors, as
revealed by the data trap, and user comments are
reasonably adequate indicators.); and

(b) the DSS be command-based, with minimal constrictions
on mode and sequence of use, to allow personalized,
innovative use (User ⟶ System)

(2) for the implementation loop:

(a) middle-out design, relying on APL to permit responsive
service (User ⟶ Designer); and

(b) close contact with users, either by one of the
development teams or a technical intermediary with
good knowledge of school finance, from within the
user organization (Designer ⟶ User)

(3) for the evolution loop:

(a) a data "trap" to monitor how individual users work
with ISSPA; and

(b) ongoing addition of new commands, expecially in
response to user requests and ideas (Designer ⟶ System);
this also requires continued research on our part.

The weakest aspect of our efforts to apply this adaptive development strategy was in the implementation loop. We frequently did not
provide adequate facilitation (Designer ⟶ User). Users need "hand-
holding" not because they are stupid or scared of the system, but because
the adaptive links, especially the cognitive loop, consistently strain
the existing system. There is a continuous state of flux. Users who

have had no trouble for months may move to more complex analysis, using
the same commands, or want to try new ones. The designer has to remain
in the loop and the middle-out process has to continue. We frequently
got phone calls from users, trying to tell us what they needed and asking
for very small adjustments to the DSS. Failure to respond in such
situations blocks learning or interrupts the users' efforts to adapt
the system to their own problem-solving.

We found that personalized usage is, as we expected, the rule
and not the exception. Every ISSPA user has an individual style.
Some are very visual and rely on graphics rather than tables, and some
continuously define new variables (e.g., (V101 + V207)/V371 = "number
of special education students per full-time teacher"). Some use ISSPA
as a report generator, others as a means of model-building. Some are
systematic and others more divergent in their problem-solving. Almost
invariably, dissatisfactions with ISSPA comes from a user's need for an
individualized system.

The good users quickly identified new commands they wanted. These
could not have been defined in advance. We spent substantial time
when the initial version was released getting a "wish list" from the
first users. However, it was the actual use of the DSS that stimulated
demands and specifications.

The success of ISSPA has depended on supporting the cognitive loop
and evolving the DSS. We anticipated this and conclude that DSS designers
should, as we did:

(1)   design the dialog first and ensure it provides an immediately
      usable, flexible and responsive system;

(2)   think in terms of verbs and commands; and

(3)   present users with a simple, clear data representation.

6. Command-Based DSS and User Verbs

The second point above is contentious and conflicts with the
recommendations of several DSS researchers. Bennett, for example,
demonstrates the value of a menu-driven approach for interactive graphics.[29]
It is easier for users to be reminded of what they can choose than to
have to specify it. A menu design minimizes the need for prior knowledge and provides familiar and recognizable options. Artman shows
how a DSS architecture can combine the merits of the menu representation
and command flexibility, using an APL-based menu generator developed
by Sigle and Howland.[30]

Our choice of command-driven system was based on both behavioral
and technical considerations:

(1) Given our concern for stimulating learning and, hence, the
use of new analytic methods, we wanted the design structure
to be directly related to the users' way of thinking.

(2) If the DSS is a collection of discrete, independent functions,
APL can be used to great advantage.

A new function in ISSPA is defined by the user in terms of:

VERB: NOUN(S): MODIFIER.

For example, RANK V401, V509 by V101. The verbs are APL functions and
the nouns are data items. There is a minimal amount of translation
from the user's concept to the technical implementation. Users understand the idea of commands; their specification is bounded by the use
of the verb, even though they may not define exact calculations and output formats.

This approach is ideally suited to middle-out design. The designer
and user sketch out the dialog and the designer produces a first cut
that can be quickly modified in response to the user's reactions.

The modifier is, conceptually, an adverb. ISSPA is command-based.
Within a command, we use a structured dialog or menu to handle sub-
options. The initial version of CORRELATE thus asked:

DO YOU WANT PARTIAL CORRELATIONS?

WHICH VARIABLE DO YOU WANT TO CONTROL FOR?

Our ideas on verbs and commands were influenced by Blanning and
Contreras.[31] Blanning takes a linguistic approach to DSS design and
aims towards a generative grammar. Contreras, following Berry, shows
how APL allows levels of language that permit a rich English-like dialog
to be built up from very simple building blocks.[32] Keen and Wagner
describe IFPS, a FORTRAN-based end-user planning language, well-suited
to DSS development.[33] IFPS is not command-based, but reflects the same
focus on specifications being given to the system via a simple syntax
based on command/verb, nouns and adverbs, that corresponds to something
in the user's head. Examples are:

(a) Contreras and Skertchly:[34]

DEFINE 'RESULTS' AS (PRICE x SALES) - (COST x INVENTORY)

COMPUTE RESULTS

DISPLAY MEDIAN PROFIT

COUNT DEMAND $>$ AVERAGE DEMAND.

DEFINE, AVERAGE, COMPUTE, DISPLAY and MEDIAN are APL functions.

(b) IFPS:

COLUMNS 4

SALES 109, 115, 1.03 * PREVIOUS SALES

.

.

WHAT IF SALES 110, 116, 1.05* PREVIOUS SALES

(c) ISSPA:

DESCRIBE TOTENRL78; AVERAGE; MEDIAN; STOP [35]

DISPLAY V101 FOR DISTRICTS

SELECTIF COUNTY = 2

The ISSPA "sentences" are less rich than the others. However, this building-block approach is easily extended. The initial version of ISSPA was a simple set of commands. Noise words (AND) and adverbial modifiers were added, e.g., CROSSTAB ... BY, DISPLAY ... PER. More recently, Gambino has extended the command syntax and developed an ISSPA planning language, which provides a model-building capability (Figure 9). Interactive Modelling and Planning System (IMPS) has grown directly out of ISSPA. This suggests that a DSS for learning and adaptive development is in effect an end-user <u>language</u> and that the verb-based structure is an elementary pidgin-English. Blanning's richer linguistic formalization and Contreras' use of APL are a natural extension of our more simple approach.

Each ISSPA command is a single "do something to something". In several instances, we later broke a command into two; CORRELATE originally included full and partial correlations. This is really two separate "do somethings". The dialog was clumsy and much of it redundant. It was easy to change the code. The main reason for the original design was that the function was taken directly from a public library. We have consistently found that APL programmers -- perhaps most programmers -- seem to pay very little attention to the connection between the user's way of thinking and the program. The dialog is often cumbersome and output formats visually cluttered and hard to follow. In integrating any function from a public library into ISSPA, we generally have to do very little to the logic, but must tidy up the dialog.

FIGURE 9: IMPS (INTERACTIVE MODELING AND PLANNING SYSTEM)

IMPS creates a file of inputs to an ISSPA run and APL
statements. This permits:

(1) Simulations to be created, quickly. (IMPS was used
     in one state to build a generalized school finance
     model in about a week.)

(2) ISSPA commands to be strung together into "exec"
     files; in the example below, line 1100 generates the
     asterisked user inputs and sequence of ISSPA
     commands.

1. IMPS Code

```
100 ₳ PROPOSAL 2 CATEGORICAL AID SET TO 0.
200 ₳ INCENTIVE AID SET TO 100 PCT MATCHING.
300 ₳VARIABLE SECTION
400     BASICAIDPUPIL←325.
500     SPECEDCLASSSIZE←12
600     SPECEDGRANT←0.
700     INCENTIVERATE←1
800     STATEEQMILLAGE←25
```

100-300
Comment lines

400-800

APL statements
creating non-ISSPA
variables which are
needed in a simulation
capability

```
 900 ᴀEQUATION SECTION
1000 CLEAR                                          1000-3900 ISSPA
1100 CHOOSE;I;V102;V104;V504;V506;STOP              command sequence
1200 ᴀCOMPUTE STATE BASIC AID
1300 DEFINE TOTADM78×BASICAIDPUPIL                  1000 clear all current
1400 STATE BASIC AID PROPOSAL 2                          active variables
1500 BASICP2
1600 STATE BASIC/AID/PROPOSAL 2
1700 F15.2
1800 ᴀCOMPUTE CATEGORICAL AID (SPECIAL ED.)
1900 DEFINE SPECEDGRANT×(0⌈SPECEDADM78÷SPECEDCLASSSIZE)
2000 CATEGORICAL AID PROPOSAL 2
2100 CATEGORICALP2
2200 CATEGORICAL/AID/PROPOSAL 2
2300 F15.2
2400 ᴀCOMPUTE INCENTIVE AID
2500 DEFINE INCENTIVERATE×(.001×0⌈V504-STATEEQMILLAGE)×V506
2600 STATE INCENTIVE AID PROPOSAL 2
2700 INCENTIVEP2
2800 INCENTIVE/AID/PROPOSAL 2
2900 F15.2
3000 ᴀCOMPUTE TOTAL STATE AID UNDER PROPOSAL
3100 DEFINE BASICP2 + CATEGORICALP2 + INCENTIVEP2
3200 TOTAL STATE AID UNDER PROPOSAL 2
3300 TOTAIDP2
3400 TOTAL STATE/AID/PROPOSAL 2
3500 F15.2
3600 ᴀDISPLAY SECTION
3700 DISPLAY BASICP2,CATEGORICALP2,INCENTIVEP2 FOR DISTRICTS
3800 *SAMPLE
3900 STOP
```

2. Part of the IMPS Run

* COMMAND: CLEAR   (line 1000)

* COMMAND: CHOOSE   (line 1100)

* GROUP OR ITEM?   I

* ENTER VARIABLE TO BE CHOSEN ('STOP) V102
*   V104
                                           V504
                                           V506
                                           STOP

COMMAND: ∗COMPUTE STATE BASIC AID   (line 1200)

                                              (lines 1300 – 1700)

COMMAND: DEFINE TOTADM78×BASICAIDPUPIL

ENTER IDENTIFIER: STATE BASIC AID PROPOSAL 2

ENTER SYNONYM (ONE WORD--NO BLANKS): BASICP2

ENTER PRINT LABEL: STATE BASIC/AID/PROPOSAL 2

ENTER FORMAT CODE: F15.2   (run for lines 1800 –
                                             3500 omitted here)

           :

COMMAND: ∗DISPLAY SECTION   (line 3600)

COMMAND: DISPLAY BASICP2,CATEGORICALP2,INCENTIVEP2 FOR DISTRICTS   (3700)
DISTRICT (STOP):   ∗SAMPLE   (3800)
DISTRICT (STOP):   STOP   (3900)
∗PP∗

	STATE BASIC AID PROPOSAL 2	CATEGORICAL AID PROPOSAL 2	INCENTIVE AID PROPOSAL 2
∗			
1. 0102 BEACHWOOD CITY S.D.	522,925.00	0.00	3,584,334.
2. 0301 BIG CITY S.D.	35,874,475.00	0.00	62,380,435.7
3. 0501 CAPITOL CITY S.D.	28,269,962.50	0.00	15,687,347.47
4. 0504 GRANDVIEW HEIGHTS	456,950.00	0.00	672,362.03
5. 0401 HUNTINGTON LOCAL S.D	406,006.25	0.00	35,944.39
6. 0403 MIAMI EAST LOCAL S.D	526,743.75	0.00	227,183.
7. 0106 MONROEVILLE LOCAL	253,012.50	0.00	391,538.8
8. 0207 WINDHAM EX VILL S.D.	512,443.75	0.00	311,104.9
9. 0206 XENIA CITY S.D.	2,201,550.00	0.00	1,282,141.5

∗IM∗

A useful additional benefit of a command-based design is that
one may disguise the DSS. We can make ISSPA look like a simple reporting
system by not informing users that commands such as REGRESS, CROSSTABS
and EQUITY exist. Similarly, we can present it as a statistical package. More importantly, we can hide and later reveal commands. For
example, we designed several simple functions for exploratory data
analysis (Tukey). They can be incorporated into the system and brought
to the attention of individual users when the time seems right. A command becomes apparent only when it is used. Already, we have developed
commands specifically for an individual user. These are part of ISSPA
but not revealed to all users.

The commands relate to learning and evolution. The adaptive
development strategy also implies a level of representation of user
behavior, design criteria and system functions. We need a common and
comparable methodology for:

(1) descriptive mapping: at a global level, one could
capture users' problem-solving in terms of, say
cognitive style (McKenney & Keen, Henderson)[36] or at
a micro-level in terms of uses of visual images.
Neither level of analysis, however, provides clear
design criteria for a DSS.

(2) prescriptive mapping: here again, one might define
an optimal decision process in terms of an overall
logic (e.g., decision theory, linear programming) or,
at the micro-level, in relation to individual decision
rules. There is no link in either case with the
descriptive map.

(3) DSS design structure: a macro-level representation
is a set of program (or model) specifications, and
the micro-level, the program logic. There is no
link here with the maps of the task and user processes.

An intermediate level permits comparability and integration.
User verbs, correspond to subtasks and translate into commands.
Figure 10 extends the adaptive design framework to include task
representation. Adaptive design involves describing decision processes
in terms of verbs, tracking user learning in relation to the use of
commands and the verbs they reflect (and vice versa), and evolving
new commands. Learning can really only be monitored in relation to
the concrete evidence provided by the data trap.

The command-verb link is thus the means by which an understanding
of the decision situation is translated into system functions and their
use observed in order to extend the DSS. We find the use of command-
verb as the discrete unit of analysis and design to be convenient,
reliable and informative.

We are currently analyzing longitudinal data collected by the
data trap. Essentially, this involves a form of protocol analysis.
The data support our initial expectations that:

(1) Usage of ISSPA will be personalized; there is no
overall pattern across users;

(2) Each user will develop consistent command sequences,
for a given task. A sequence might be, for regression
analysis:

(a) SCATTER, get a scatter diagram;

(b) CORRELATE;

FIGURE 10:   TASK REPRESENTATION IN ADAPTIVE DESIGN

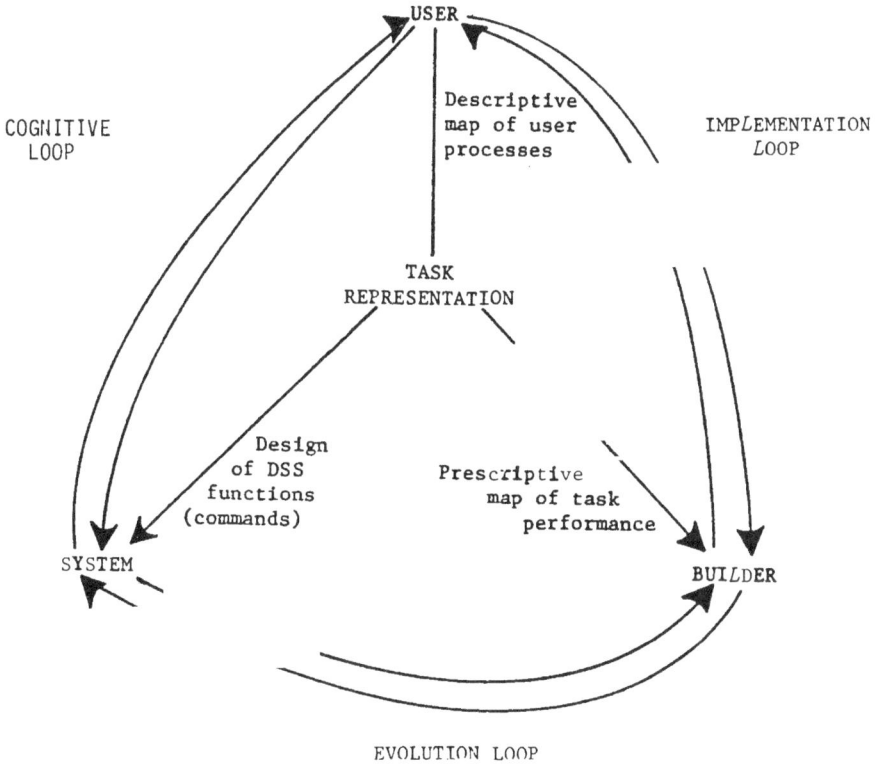

(c) REGRESS;

(d) DESCRIBE residuals.

This sequence reflects a coherent approach to analysis, largely stimulated by the DSS.

(3) The scope of analysis will be broadened; this is indicated by the use of the more "prescriptive" commands, manipulation of variables and idiosyncratic sequences reflecting a concept, heuristic or personal strategy.

The data trap records user identification, day, time, and ISSPA command. It is simple and informative. With one user, for instance, we tracked over a two-week period, a shift from correlation analysis and tabular displays with limited manipulation of variables (via the DEFINE command) to:

(1) Examine outliers and divide the distribution into discrete groupings (e.g., deciles).

(2) Analysis of selected districts, grouping districts into categories.

(3) Weighting individual groups, and manipulating the grouped variables.

From both research on DSS and our own experience, we strongly conclude that a command-based strategy is natural for DSS development. It clarifies how to look at the users' process, before and with the DSS, how to design and evolve the system and how to evaluate it. What is missing at present is a clear theory of user learning. There is a gap between the descriptive and prescriptive decision process; bridging it is a rather haphazard process at present.

7. APL and the Mythical Man-Month

The preceding two sections discuss aspects of program design
rather than programming. DSS do not involve any distinctive technology,
they use FORTRAN, APL, CRT's, standard data management concepts, etc.,
and are frequently small in scale. They imply, however, a particular
programming style. The main reason many DSS designers advocate the
use of APL is their concern for:

(1) fast delivery of the system;

(2) the ability to restructure the DSS at short notice;

(3) direct and responsive service to users; and

(4) reducing the fixed costs of program development and
     making it a marginal cost venture.

The first three of these points follow from the principles
of adaptive design. Middle-out, in particular, relies on fast delivery
and fast modifications; all momentum and credibility are lost if users
have to wait for a month for response. Case studies of DSS (see Keen,
Alter)[37] emphasize these issues, particularly the value of having a prototype system being made available at a low cost to demonstrate the
feasibility and value of the DSS. Quite often, these prototypes are
"bootlegged"; the design team spends one or two weeks rushing to get
a system up while management is still discussing the business problem
and their options. Low cost is essential in such a situation. Management clearly is unlikely to approve a $50,000 investment to try out
the designers' ideas: the prototype is, after all, only a first-cut,
a hypothesis and an experiment.

One of the major blockages to the application of computer technology to management decision making over the past decade has surely
been the high fixed costs of programming. Data processing departments

cannot respond to ad hoc requests for small reports or simple analysis.
Any COBOL program is likely to involve a month to write and test, even
when the logic is simple. Similarly, changes an existing program
are surprisingly expensive (surprising to the client). Often, they
are not even feasible, because they require major changes to the existing program structure.

Adaptive design and evolution are likely to succeed only if DSS
development involves low fixed costs. Developing the initial system
and adding a new command should require only an incremental investment,
where the main cost is the programmer's charge per hour.

The cost function for program development is basically:

$$Cost = F + (PH \times PR) + (MH \times MR) + (UH \times UR)$$

where:

(1) F is the fixed cost of logic design, housekeeping
and system set up (e.g., JCL, ENVIRONMENT DIVISION
statements in COBOL); this is basically independent
of the application;

(2) PH is number of programmer hours and PR the cost
per hour;

(3) MH and MR are the machine hours (for testing and
trial use) and cost per hour; and

(4) UH and UR are the users' time and costs.

In traditional data processing applications, F is high, and the
costs for machine time and user time relatively low. The programmer
cost per hour for COBOL is also low in relation to that for really
outstanding programmers working in, say, a marketing staff unit or as
consultants. PH is generally high.

The costs are very different in DSS applications. PR will be high since:

(1) middle-out and descriptive and prescriptive mapping require an understanding the decision making context; the designer has to be able to relate well to and interact with relatively senior managers and professionals; the average systems analyst and COBOL programmer lacks the training or interest for this;

(2) if a system is to be built quickly, the programmer has to be far more productive than the average data processing professional; and

(3) the importance of a clear program architecture, flexible structure, functional generality, and responsive interface requires that the programmer have experience with on-line applications, and strong skills in programming techniques. Much of the adaptive development strategy is similar to top-down design, structured programming and stepwise refinement. These tools for improving software productivity are not easy to learn: EDP Analyzer reports that programmers need to be "converted .... and very likely they will resist the new techniques at first".[38]

If PR is high, PH needs to be low. Moreover, DSS development
requires users to be directly involved. Grajew and Tolovi found that
the number of hours required -- using middle-out -- is not high (less
than 50 hours spread over 16 weeks) but whereas "users" in data processing applications are generally junior to middle-level clerical personnel
and supervisors, with DSS they are higher-paid managers or professionals,
who also have little time available. Reducing PH helps reduce UH.

The attractiveness of APL for many designers follows from the
trade-offs it allows among components of the cost function. F is
negligible, particularly using a command-based structure; in general,
one can "bread-board" a system and get started quickly. APL relieves
the programmer of set-up charges such as dimensioning arrays, and
declaring variable types of data names. PH is dramatically reduced;
a given piece of program logic can be coded in about one-tenth of the
time required with FORTRAN. With a DSS, much of the existing code
at any stage will later be rewritten; this is especially true with
the initial version of the system. The language is compact, with one
APL line equivalent to 6-15 lines of FORTRAN.

With APL, the cost function becomes:

    a low fixed cost (F) + low programmer hours (PH) x
    high programmer cost per hour + high machine cost +
    relatively high user costs (UH x UR).

If delivery time is a key factor, then obviously users will be ready
to pay a premium in terms of PR to reduce PH.

With APL, one must accept relatively high machine costs. Middle-
out implies a fairly continuous cycle:

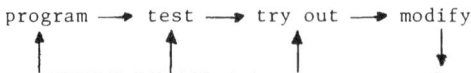

program ⟶ test ⟶ try out ⟶ modify

The process is inefficient in terms of machine usage. Machine costs
per hour are likely to be high for several reasons:

(1) APL is an interpretive language.

(2) An interactive system must provide good response time;
     this often is possible only with a high quality,
     expensive time-shared system, especially if, as with
     ISSPA, there are operations on large matrices.

(3) A good user can do a great deal of work in an hour
     with a well-designed DSS.

Cheap APL services are available. Too often, however, they are
unreliable and overloaded. Cadillac service is not cheap.

It is extremely unlikely that we could have built the initial
version of ISSPA without APL. With middle-out design, every day counts.
Much of the interaction between designer and user involves trying out
ideas at the terminal. In several instances, we responded to a user's
request on the spot. For example, one analyst wanted to know if we
could provide a PERCENT function. Ten minutes later -- and three lines
of APL -- there it was. An interpretive language facilitates such
development.

The specter of the mythical man-month loomed over us throughout
the development process. Brooks' warning for software designers is:

(1) When the code is written, 10% of the work is done.

(2) As program complexity grows by x, programming effort
     increases by x^a, where the exponent a is estimated by
     Nanus and Farr and by Weinwurm[39] to be about 1.5:

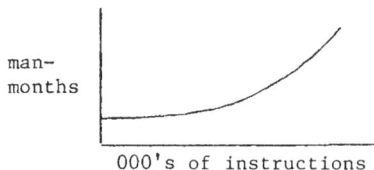

000's of instructions

(3)   Much of the incremental 90% of the effort involves
      testing and integration.

We believed that using APL would enable us to:

(1)   reduce the time needed for the 10%;

(2)   borrow from public libraries, thus reducing testing;

(3)   break the program up into small, discrete units
      so that x^a is close to x;

(4)   integrate new routines easily; and

(5)   reduce program errors.

In general, our expectations were met. We encountered three main
types of problems, all of which had a significant impact on development
time and costs:

(1)   As the use of ISSPA became more complex and new functions
      were added, interaction errors were introduced; Command A
      works perfectly, as does Command B, but used in sequence,
      they generate a bug, often an elusive one.

(2)   Far more resources were needed for the user-system dialog
      than for the logic of the commands.

(3)   The initial commands permitted us simple "sentences".
      Evolution, user learning and the addition of user-defined
      commands result in -- intendedly so -- more complex ones.
      It then became essential to introduce consistent system
      conventions and add system commands. These do not add
      to the functional capabilities of the system and diverted
      resources from the evolution of user commands.

(4)   Machine costs were far higher than expected and the code
      was "opaque".

Brooks' response to the first three points might well be,
"I told you so.". He did. We thought we could finesse the problems
implicit in Figure 1. Almost certainly, we still saved substantial
time and effort by using APL but the pattern Brooks identifies seems
to hold as much for ISSPA as for data processing projects. Coding is
still 10% of the effort.

This point is not discussed much in work on either APL or DSS.
Many, perhaps most, model-based DSS described in case studies are
either for ad hoc use, in which case there is no need to make them
into products, or the work is done by high-quality, low cost programmers
working in universities. Clearly, APL is very effective for ad hoc
systems.

The interaction errors often related to problems with internal
pointers and multiple copies of matrices which are not consistent. As
we elaborated the "syntax" of ISSPA, several commands would be used
within other commands. To the user, the structure remained simple;
indeed, the whole aim in designing the user-system dialog was to ensure
ISSPA be easy to use even by someone with no prior experience with
computer systems. Internally, however, the structure grew exponentially
more complex. This was also true for the data management routines.

The interaction errors were sometimes hard to trace. Errors in
the logic of a user command were quickly found. As mentioned earlier,
users played a key role in locating unobtrusive errors, ones which the
programmer is unlikely to spot. Their expertise in school finance com-
bined with initiative, intelligence, and interest in ISSPA significantly
affected the technical quality of the DSS.

While the use of routines from public libraries clearly reduced
testing time, since they are already debugged, we had to spend substantial

effort in improving the user-system dialog. For example, the
FREQUENCIES command took two hours to integrate and check out and
almost twenty hours to redesign the dialog. Many programmers seem to
have little sense of aesthetics. Figure 11 shows a sample output
from an APL-based DSS that the designer regards as easy to use
and well-suited to managers' needs. It is fairly typical of the
style of most of the routines we took from public libraries, and
does not meet the standard of dialog we view as critical for DSS.
The output table is not self-explanatory, the abbreviations seem
unnecessary (QTY for QUANTITY) and the spacing poor.

Ness argues that a DSS cannot be made more useful by adding
"cosmetics".[40] Our view is very different, and seems to be supported
by users' reactions. We felt that a DSS has be be seen as a personal
tool and a mundane one. "Mundane" is hard to define here; it means
easy to live with, quickly integrated into one's ongoing activities
and then, in a way, taken for granted. A calculator is personal and
mundane in this sense. "Cosmetics" are an important aspect of mundane-
ness. The quality of the read-out display, the size of the buttons,
the location of functions, etc., make a particular calculator easy to
live with. An indication of one's satisfaction with it is that it is
taken for granted. With some calculators, one's attention is drawn
to very minor inconveniences or cosmetic flaws.

We felt, and still do, that for a DSS product, cosmetics are
important. The dialog in Figure 11 may be acceptable to a person with
a technical bent but not to most others. We went to great lengths
to build a mundane system. For example, the DESCRIBE command produces
descriptive statistics, including the standard deviation and variance
of a variable. If the variance is too large for the output field,

FIGURE 11: EXAMPLE OF APL DIALOG

```
SELECTION:PROD=CHAIR∧CITY=ATL,BOS,CHI
FUNCTION:CROSS
ROW CLASS 1 (OR ROW FIELD):CITY
COL CLASS 1 (OR COL FIELD):QTY≤10
COL CLASS 2:=11_50
COL CLASS 3:>50
COL CLASS 4:
TAB FIELD:PRICE×QTY
PERCENTAGES (Y OR N):Y
PAGE NO. 1
```

```
12:35        4/20/77        APL DATA INTERFACE
DEMOSALES VFILE;PROD0='CHAIR'∧PROD1=' '∧CITY=ATL,BOS,CHI ;CROSS:
             TAB:PRICE×QTY
```

		QTY		
CITY	C1	C2	C3	TOTAL
	→ .57	→ .43	→ .00	
ATL	9340	7110	0	16450
	↓ .35	↓ .17	↓ .00	↓ .17
	→ .20	→ .57	→ .22	
BOS	8300	23570	9240	41110
	↓ .31	↓ .58	↓ .35	↓ .44
	→ .24	→ .28	→ .48	
CHI	8810	10250	17500	36560
	↓ .33	↓ .25	↓ .65	↓ .39
	→ .28	→ .43	→ .28	→ 1.00
TOTAL	26450	40930	26740	94120

⟶ = row percentages

↓ = column percentages

initially asterisks were printed. This is a convention familiar to
FORTRAN users but makes no sense. The variance is not **********.
While a policy analyst will get used to asterisks appearing on a report,
a legislator will wonder why the computer made a mistake. We decided
to substitute the words VERY LARGE. Similarly, if the variable has
no mode, we printed NONE instead of 0.

In several states, we did not make any presentation of ISSPA
to senior administrators in the users' organization. The users did so;
it was their system, not ours. They almost invariably emphasized the
"cosmetics", which they viewed as a reflection of our willingness
to tailor ISSPA to their needs. To an extent, functional capabilities
are taken as a given. A calculator multiplies and divides; the issue
is how well does it do so, which translates to how "mundane" it is.

In retrospect, we needed to carry the concepts of "verbs" and
commands further than we did in the initial design. ISSPA has become
in effect an end-user language. It involves a simple grammar, which
includes modifiers and conjunctions. The conventions must be consistent
and easy to learn. We had minor, but unnecessary problems with
prepositions. For example, the CROSSTAB, RANK, EQUITY, NTILES, WAVERAGE
(weighted average), and SCATTER commands all require a 'by', 'with', or
'versus'. We initially did not take into account the fact that as
commands evolve from simple generic verbs to user-defined routines,
prepositions and modifiers become more necessary and frequently used.
The surface texture of the dialog has be be graceful, consistent and
lucid. This obviously takes careful design; even though the programming
is simple, it takes up more time than does coding the user commands.

For similar reasons, we increasingly had to commit resources to
developing system commands, which either increased flexibility of the

DSS or provided help and information about ISSPA.

    WHAT IS Vxxx

    SYNONYM; this allows the user to change a variable

        label or identifier.

    LABEL; for improving readability of reports.

    COMMAND COST

    SESSION COST

    CONTINUE (originally named LUNCH); this allows the

        user to log-off and restart at the same point.

All these commands were developed in response to user requests
or problems. The design structure made it easy to integrate them and
they involved small increments of effort. However, at one point, we
had to hire a junior programmer to handle them and for some time were
not able to keep up with our user's growing demands for such add-on
features.

Our initial estimate of the cost to run ISSPA was $40 an hour.
We used a high-quality time-sharing service with its own private
telecommunications network, which permitted total portability. We
could work from Philadelphia with users in California, Ohio or
Michigan and provide fast response. Database creation involved, of
course, shipping a tape to where the host computer is located.

Actual costs were far higher, often as high as $200 an hour.
The program code was written lucidly and simply, avoiding the typical
APL-freak's habit of trying to get a whole program into a single line
of code. We expected that when ISSPA became a product, we would have
to tidy up the code. We soon found that APL heavily penalizes careless
programming. An equation calculating a value for 600 school districts
cost $160 written one way and $20 written another. The rules change
as the DSS becomes a product. The need at the start is fast development

which requires "brute force" programming and close attention to the users' needs and perspective. At the product stage, one has to inspect the code.

At one point, we felt that machine costs would be reduced by completely rewriting the code. We contracted with the company whose APL services we were using; they felt sure they could reduce the cost by 50% and spent six weeks "optimizing" the code. There was virtually no improvement; the original code was, on the whole, just as efficient.

Perhaps, as more experience is gained with APL, this problem of "opaqueness" will be resolved, but we were surprised -- expensively so -- by the extent to which highly experienced APL programmers have little insight into the relationship between the source code and machine performance. They do not need this insight for an ad hoc DSS or one used only intermittently. Obviously, as machine costs decrease, the cost problem we encountered will disappear. However, with any computer product, some effort to optimize efficiency is necessary. We suspect that this will be difficult for "problem-oriented" higher level languages for at least the next few years.

Despite these problems, associated not so much with the development as with the consolidation of ISSPA, APL provided the expected advantages. In particular, the programming cost for a new user command is indeed incremental with an extremely low fixed component. For one user, we developed a major new command, which was based on ideas he had got from using ISSPA and which added an important policy concept to school finance analysis. It was "working" in a day; he estimated that at best, it would take three months for the state education programmer's department to implement a similar capability. He was quite willing to put up with minor blemishes in the routine in exchange for such responsive service.

We estimate that about 800 programmer hours of effort have gone into ISSPA. Of course, the system is much more powerful than the initial version, but even so, the figure is painfully close to Brooks' estimate that the final development effort will be nine times the coding effort.

From the few case studies which describe the extension of a DSS to a product, it is clear, in retrospect, that our experiences are fairly typical (see, for example, Alter's discussion of a DSS for media planning).[41] We have given this paper the subtitle of the Mythical Man-Month Revisited. Six months ago, we assumed it would be the Mythical Man-Month Defeated.

8. <u>Conclusion: Guidelines for Building DSS</u>

In Section 1, we stated that one aim in developing ISSPA was to see if the DSS field is now at a point where one can define reliable guidelines for building DSS. Obviously, our experiences are not generalizable. Nonetheless, they confirm much of the often implicit principles of DSS design and the explicit findings of DSS research. We thus feel that we can make some fairly strong assertions:

   (1) Adaptive design is essential; any systems analyst,
        programmer or consultant who wants to build DSS
        has to know how to:

        (a) <u>get started</u>: DSS applications do not
             come tidily packaged with neat spec-
             ifications. The middle-out approach
             provides a means of learning from
             and responding to the user;

        (b) <u>respond quickly</u>: A DSS is equivalent
             to a system for evolution and learning.

The design structure and programming techniques must facilitate this.

(c) <u>pay close attention to user-system interfaces and outputs</u>: A DSS is a set of relatively simple components that must fit together to permit complex, varied and idiosyncratic problem-solving. The designer needs to get a very detailed understanding of the task to be supported and of the people who carry out the task. The natural sequence and order of priority in DSS development is:

(1) design the dialog;

(2) design the commands in terms of the <u>users</u>' processes and concepts;

(3) define what the <u>user</u> does and sees when this command is invoked; and

(4) work backwards to program logic and data management.

(2) <u>The architecture of a DSS is critical</u>. It must be built on the assumption that there will be substantial evolution and that flexibility is essential.

(3) The development process must be based on techniques and design structures that <u>reduce the fixed costs of programming and the time to respond to users</u>. The trade-offs are complex, and we suffered badly from the high machine costs we incurred in gaining low programmer costs.

(4) <u>Data management involves high software overhead</u> and
     is the major source of complex program errors.

(5) <u>A good user is essential</u>. As one ISSPA user stated
     "After working with a DSS, at a certain point, it
     takes on a life of its own.". The DSS is man-with-
     machine; the machine alone is not enough.

The final point to be made is a rueful one. There is indeed
no free lunch. The demands in time and effort for delivering a DSS
product are as high as for any computer system. The process is more
flexible and early progress often dramatically excitingly faster
than for traditional data-processing applications, but the 9x still
holds.

APPENDIX 1:   EXAMPLES OF ISSPA ROUTINES

(Based on problem set in user manual;
CHOOSE commands omitted)

1. Prepare a table showing the surplus (deficit) of 1978 special
    education revenues over expenditures.

    COMMAND: DEFINE SPECEDAID78 - SPECEDEXP78

    ENTER VARIABLE NAME: SPECIAL EDUCATION SURPLUS 78

    ENTER SYNONYM (ONE WORD--NO BLANKS): SPECEDSURPLUS78

    ENTER PRINT LABEL: SPEC. ED./SURPLUS/1978

    ENTER FORMAT CODE: I10

    NEW VARIABLE DEFINED.   ACTIVE VARIABLE NO.: A7

    COMMAND: LIST SPECEDAID78, SPECEDEXP78,SPECEDSURPLUS78

    COLUMN FOOTINGS:?   YES
    COLUMNS:?   ALL
    COMPUTATION TECHNIQUE:?   TOTALS
    FOOTING TITLE: (<CR>=NO TITLE.):
    ◦PP◦

			SPEC. ED. AID 1978	SPEC. ED. OP. EXP. 1979	SPEC. ED. SURPLUS 1978
1.	0102	ADAMS	50,800	47,872	2,928
2.	0503	BRADLEY	134,400	124,068	10,332
3.	0101	CAPITOL CITY	347,600	354,268	⁻6,668
4.	0301	DULLES CITY	1,309,600	1,266,272	43,328
5.	0501	EASTERN CITY	539,200	504,488	34,712
6.	0201	FRANKLIN	89,600	91,770	⁻2,170
7.	0202	GARFIELD	93,600	90,337	3,263
8.	0504	HURON	0	0	0
9.	0401	IONA	280,400	285,285	⁻4,885
10.	0203	JEFFERSON	70,000	65,110	4,890
11.	0107	KIRKMAN	145,200	136,175	9,025
12.	0204	LAWRENCE	188,400	174,801	13,599
13.	0402	MONROE	34,400	33,030	1,370
14.	0205	NEEDHAM	110,400	104,641	5,759
15.	0403	ONTARIO	46,000	43,004	2,996
16.	0103	PARKINGTON	140,000	140,861	⁻861
17.	0106	QUEENS	20,400	19,790	610
18.	0210	ROOSEVELT	0	0	0
19.	0209	SUPERIOR	48,400	46,936	⁻1,464
20.	0502	THREE RIVERS CITY	403,200	406,822	⁻3,622
21.	0208	UPLAND	134,800	137,831	⁻3,031
22.	0207	VILLA PARK	42,000	41,651	349
23.	0105	WALNUT GROVE	17,200	16,231	969
24.	0206	YARDLEY	152,400	151,601	799
25.	0104	ZELLERBACH	134,400	137,086	2,686
			4,532,400	4,419,927	112,473

COMMAND:

2. Prepare a table showing 1978 total enrollment and expenditures per pupil for all districts with 5,000 or more pupils.

COMMAND: _DEFINE TOTOPEXP78÷TOTENRL78_

ENTER VARIABLE NAME: _OPERATING EXPENDITURES PER PUPIL 78_

ENTER SYNONYM (ONE WORD--NO BLANKS): _EXPPUPIL78_

ENTER PRINT LABEL: _EXPENDITURES/PER PUPIL/1978_

ENTER FORMAT CODE: _I15_

NEW VARIABLE DEFINED. ACTIVE VARIABLE NO.: A18

COMMAND: _SELECTIF TOTENRL78≥5000_
ENTER DESCRIPTION OF SELECTION: _LARGE SCHOOL DISTRICTS_
SELECTION IN EFFECT
10   UNITS CURRENTLY SELECTED

DO YOU WISH TO SEE UNITS CURRENTLY SELECTED?   _NO_

COMMAND: _LIST TOTENRL78,EXPPUPIL78_
COLUMN FOOTINGS:?   _N_
∘PP∘

		TOTAL ENROLLMENT 1978	EXPENDITURES PER PUPIL 1978
1.	0503 BRADLEY	6,160	1,576
2.	0101 CAPITOL CITY	10,859	1,135
3.	0301 DULLES CITY	38,720	1,568
4.	0501 EASTERN CITY	16,331	1,246
5.	0401 IONA	8,243	1,059
6.	0107 KIRKMAN	6,229	1,199
7.	0204 LAWRENCE	7,750	1,462
8.	0502 THREE RIVERS CITY	12,505	2,042
9.	0206 YARDLEY	6,773	1,185
10.	0104 ZELLERBACH	6,064	1,157

3. Prepare a table showing the absolute and percent increase in average teacher salaries between 1978 and 1979 for the following districts:

Bradley - Needham - Huron - Franklin - Roosevelt - Lawrence -

Yardley - Parkington

COMMAND: *DEFINE* 100×(AVGSAL79-AVGSAL78)÷AVGSAL78

ENTER VARIABLE NAME: *PCT CHANGE AVERAGE SALARY 78*

ENTER SYNONYM (ONE WORD--NO BLANKS): *CHGAVGSAL7879*

ENTER PRINT LABEL: *PCT. CHANGE/AVG. SALARY/1978-1979*

ENTER FORMAT CODE: *F11.1*

NEW VARIABLE DEFINED. ACTIVE VARIABLE NO.: A23

COMMAND: *SELECT UNITS*
UNIT ('STOP'): *BRADLEY*
UNIT ('STOP'): *NEEDHAM*
UNIT ('STOP'): *HURON*
UNIT ('STOP'): *FRANKLIN*
UNIT ('STOP'): *ROOSEVELT*
UNIT ('STOP'): *LAWRENCE*
UNIT ('STOP'): *YARDLEY*
UNIT ('STOP'): *PARKINGTON*
UNIT ('STOP'): *STOP*
ENTER DESCRIPTION OF SELECTION: 8 *DISTRICTS CHOSEN AT RANDOM*
SELECTION IN EFFECT
8 *UNITS CURRENTLY SELECTED*

COMMAND: *RANK AVGSAL79,AVGSAL78,CHGAVGSAL7879 BY CHGAVGSAL7879*
ORDER (ASCENDING OR DECENDING):? *DESCENDING*
COLUMN FOOTINGS:? *N*
•PP•

			AVG TEACHER SALARY 1979	AVG TEACHER SALARY 1978	PCT. CHANGE AVG. SALARY 1978-1979
1.	0204	LAWRENCE	14,071	12,100	16.3
2.	0205	NEEDHAM	10,827	9,885	9.5
3.	0210	ROOSEVELT	11,614	11,116	4.5
4.	0103	PARKINGTON	13,060	12,775	2.2
5.	0504	HURON	13,799	13,580	1.6
6.	0201	FRANKLIN	12,003	11,820	1.5
7.	0206	YARDLEY	12,160	12,001	1.3
8.	0503	BRADLEY	MISSING	12,699	MISSING

4. How many districts had 1978 total revenue per pupil greater than
   $1,500? How many districts had 1978 revenue greater than $1,500,
   but received no state basic aid in 1978? Which districts were
   they?

   COMMAND: DEFINE TOTREV78 + TOTENRL78

   ENTER VARIABLE NAME: TOTAL REVENUE PER PUPIL 1978

   ENTER SYNONYM (ONE WORD--NO BLANKS): TOTREVPUP78

   ENTER PRINT LABEL: TOTAL REV/PER PUPIL/1978

   ENTER FORMAT CODE: I10

   NEW VARIABLE DEFINED. ACTIVE VARIABLE NO.: A9

   COMMAND: COUNTIF TOTREVPUP78 >1500

   8 UNITS SATISFY CONDITION(S).

   DO YOU WISH TO SEE THE UNITS?   NO

   COMMAND: COUNTIF (TOTREVPUP78 > 1500) ∧ (STATEAID78 = 0)

   5 UNITS SATISFY CONDITION(S).

   DO YOU WISH TO SEE THE UNITS?   YES

       1 0102 *ADAMS*
       2 0503 *BRADLEY*
       3 0202 *GARFIELD*
       4 0209 *SUPERIOR*
       5 0105 *WALNUT GROVE*

N O T E S

1. ISSPA is suited to any application where the data consist of a set of planning units (e.g., school districts, employees, buildings or states) and where the analysis involves aggregating, selecting and reporting some or all of the units. For example, ISSPA is likely to be used in the near future as a DSS for planning and analysis of personnel data and for tracking and evaluation of federal research grants.

2. F. P. Brooks, The Mythical Man Month, Addison-Wesley, 1977. Brooks' book is surely the best single discussion of software engineering. There is not room in this paper to do justice to its scope and insight. It covers, among other topics: (1) the distinction between programs and programming systems products (the main topic of this chapter), (2) the non-linear relationship between program size and development effort, (3) the problems of coordination in large-scale software development efforts, (4) the importance of program architecture, (5) the need for independent certification and testing of software, (6) the need for sharp tools (including APL), (7) disciplines for debugging and documentation.

   Brooks was the project manager for OS/360, the operating system for IBM's third generation. Between 1963-1966, about 500 man-years of effort went into OS/360, and at one point over 1000 people were working on it. Brooks' book is both an analysis of what happened and a recommendation of how to avoid similar programming "tar pits".

3. See Garms, Guthrie and Pierce (1978).

4. We have added a third dimention, years, so that future versions of ISSPA
    will include capability for time series analysis.

5. Most ISSPA users work with either a subset of about eight variables or
    begin by pulling in a larger number that they then aggregate or combine,
    using the DEFINE command. A dilemma for DSS designers is how to
    efficiently and quickly extract the small number of variables a user
    wants to work with from what is often a very large data base.

6. P. G. W. Keen, "Decision Support Systems: Translating Useful Models
    into Usable Techniques", Sloan Management Review, Summer 1980.

7. The Gini coefficient and Lorenz curves are standard measures of
    disparity of income or wealth. See Garms, et al.

8. Our colleague David G. Clark joined us in developing ISSPA around
    this point. He has played a major role in translating ISSPA from a
    program to a product, especially in the areas of training,
    documentation and marketing.

9. David A. Ness, who has probably been the most important single contributor
    to DSS design techniques, developed the term "middle-out" to describe
    this approach. Middle-out development (in contrast to top-down and
    botton-up) relies on prototyping, "breadboarding" and designing-by-using.
    Ness's ideas and experience have been a major influence on our work.

10. Courbon and his colleagues have carefully tracked the costs of DSS
    development and provide tetailed data on the manager's and designer's
    time involved.

11. James Phelps, Associate Superintendent in the Department of Education in
    Michigan and William Harrison, Legislative Assistant to the Education Review
    Committee in Ohio, were invaluable to us. The literature on the need for user

involvement in systems development seems to have a very passive concept. In adaptive design, the user is active and indispensable. **Dr.** Phelps and Dr. Harrison became <u>designers</u> of ISSPA by being responsive, creative users.

12. There should have been a manual; its absence caused occasional irritating and unnecessary problems (e.g., "is it CROSSTABS...WITH or BY?"). One problem adaptive design causes is that since the DSS is constantly evolving and version "0" is designed with change in mind, there is no stable system to document. It is thus essential to build as much of the user documentation into the DSS as is possible. One approach we are considering is to store the text of the user manual on disk so that it can be accessed directly from ISSPA.

13. P. G. W. Keen, "Decision Support Systems: A Research Perspective", CISR Papers, Sloan School of Management, MIT, 1980.

14. The literature on diffusion of innovations indicates that "early adopters" are generally part of an elite that is self confident and willing to break norms and traditions. One reason for seeking out such people as the first users of a DSS is that they are effective contacts and crusaders for the wider organization. As well as helping design the DSS, they in effect sell it.

15. See Berne (1979).

16. See Gerrity (1970), Stabell (1974), and Keen and Scott Morton (1978). All these authors point out that management science tends to focus only on prescriptive maps, ignoring the need for support. In teaching graduate students to be DSS users or designers, much of the course material must concentrate on descriptive conceptions of decision making. One cannot improve something one does not understand.

17. See Keen and Clark (1980).

18. See Keen (1980 b).

19. Tukey (1977) defines a range of innovative, mainly graphical techniques for analysts to really look at their data before committing themselves to analytic methods.

20. McNeil (1977) provides APL and FORTRAN source code for many EDA technique His output formats are generally clumsy; here again, we concentrated on making these useful routines more usable.

21. See also Mehtlie (1979).

22. See Carlson and Sutton (1974).

23. See Keen (1980 a). All references to Keen in Section 5 relate to this p

24. See Ness (1975).

25. See Keen (1975) and Bennett (1976).

26. See Brooks (1975), p. 46.

27. See Stabell (1974) and Andreoli and Steadman (1975).

28. See Keen and Clark (1977).

29. See Bennett (1977).

30. See Artman (1980) and Sigle and Howland (1979).

31. See Blanning, also Contreras (1979).

32. See Berry (1977).

33. See Keen and Wagner (1979). IFPS (Interactive Financial Planning System) is a product of Execucom, Inc., Austin, Texas.

34. See Contreras and Skertchly (1978).

35. The use of semi-colons allows users to operate in an "expert" mode where they do not have to wait for ISSPA to type out the standard instructions or questions. This enhancement was provided in response to user demand.

36. See McKenney and Keen (1974), Keen (1980 a), and Henderson.

37. See Alter (1980).

38. See EDP Analyzer, January, February, March 1979.

39. See Nanus and Farr (1964) and Weinwurm (1965).

40. See Ness (1976).

41. See Alter (1980), p. 225. This DSS was built by Ness and a colleague and illustrates middle-out in practice.

***

BIBLIOGRAPHY

Alter, Steven L., Decision Support Systems: Current Practice and
    Continuing Challenges, Addison-Wesley, Reading, MA, 1980.

Andreoli, P. and J. Steadman, "Management Decision Support Systems:
    Impact on the Decision Process," Master's thesis, M.I.T., 1975.

Artman, Ira B., "Design and Implementation of a Decision Support
    System for Hospital Space Management," MS Thesis, M.I.T., 1980.

Bennett, J., "Integrating Users and Decision Support Systems," In J.D.
    White (ed.), Proceedings of the Sixth and Seventh Annual
    Conferences of the Society for Management Information Systems,
    pp. 77-86, Ann Arbor: University of Michigan, July 1976.

_____, "User-Oriented Graphics Systems for Decision Support in
    Unstructured Tasks," IBM Research Lab, 1977.

Berne, R.M., and L. Steifel, "Concepts of Equity and their Relation-
    ship to School Finance Plans," Journal of Education Finance,
    Vol. 5, Fall 1979.

Berry, P., "The Democratization of Computing," Paper presented at
    Eleventh Symposium Nacional de Systemas Computacionales,
    Monterrey, Mexico, March 15-18, 1977.

Blanning, R., "The Functions of a Decision Support System," The
    Wharton School.

Brooks, F.P., The Mythical Man-Month, Addison-Wesley, Reading, MA, 1975.

Carlson, E.D. and J.A. Sutton, A Case Study of Non-Programmer Inter-
    active Problem-solving, IBM Research Report RJ, San Jose,
    CA, 1382, 1974.

Contreras, L., "Linguistic Design of Decision Support Systems," Un-
    published manuscript, Southern Mehtodist University, 1979,
    (to be a chapter in Bennett).

_____, and R. Skertchly, "A Conceptual Model for Interactive
    Systems," APL Users Meeting, Toronto, September, 1978.

Courbon, J.C., Grajew, J., et Tolovi, J.,Jr. "L'approche evolutive
    dans la mise en place des systemes interactifs d'aide a la
    decision," Papier de Recherche IAE - Grenoble, no. 78-02,
    Institut d'Administration des Entreprises, Universite de
    Grenoble II, Jan., 1978.

Garms, W., J.W. Guthrie, and L.C. Pierce, School Finance: The Economics and Politics of Public Education, Prentice-Hall, 1978.

Gerrity, T.P., Jr., "The Design of Man-Machine Decision Systems," Ph.D dissertation, M.I.T., 1970.

Grajew, J., and J. Tolovi, Jr., "Conception et mise en oeuvre des systems interactifs d'aide a la decision: l'approche evolutive," Ph.D thesis, 1978, Universite de Grenoble.

Henderson, John, "Experimental Studies of Decision Support Systems," work in progress, Florida State University.

Keen, P.G.W., "Computer-Based Decision Aids: The Evaluation Problem," Sloan Management Review, vol. 16, no. 3, pp. 17-29, Spring 1975.

_____, "Computer Systems for Top Managers: A Modest Proposal," Sloan Management Review, vol. 18, no. 1, pp.1-17, Fall 1976.

_____, "Decision Support Systems: A Research Perspective," CISR Paper, Sloan School of Management, 1980a.

_____, "Decision Support Systems: Translating Useful Models into Usable Technologies," Sloan Management Review, Summer 1980b.

_____, and D.G. Clark, "Computer Systems and Models for School Finance Policy Making: A Conceptual Framework," research report to the Ford Foundation, August 1978.

_____,"Simulations for School Finance, Survey and Assessment," research report to the Ford Foundation, 1980.

_____, and J. Wagner, "DSS: An Executive Mind Support System," DATAMATION, November, 1979.

McKenney, J.L. and P.G.W. Keen, "How Managers' Minds Work," Harvard Business Review, Vol. 52, no. 3, pp. 79-90, May-June 1974.

McNeil, D.R., Interactive Data Analysis, Wiley - Interscience, 1977.

Methlie, L., "Data Management for Decision Support Systems," Unpublished Paper, Norwegian School of Economics and Business Administration, 1979. (for Bennett book)

Nanus, B. and L. Farr, "Some cost contributors to large-scale programs," AFIPS Procedings SJCC, 25 (Spring 1964), pp. 239-248.

Ness, D., "Interactive Systems: Theories of Design," Joint Wharton/ONR Conference - Interactive Information and DSS, Dept. of Decision Sciences, The Wharton School, University of Pennsylvania, Nov. 1975.

Sigle, J. and J. Howland, "Structured Development of Menu Driven
      Application Systems," APL QUOTE QUAD '79, ACM, June 1979.

Stabell, C., "On the Development of the Decision Sypport Systems as
      a Marketing Problem," Paper presented at the International
      Federation for Information Processing Congress, Stockholm,
      Sweden, August 1974b.

Tukey, J., Exploratory Data Analysis, Addison-Wesley, 1977.

Weinwurm, G.F., "Research in the management of computer programming,"
      Report SP-2059, System Development Corp., Santa Monica, 1965.

Date Due

CPSIA information can be obtained
at www.ICGtesting.com
Printed in the USA
BVHW04*2032230718

522415BV00008B/24/P